Elizabeth of York
and the Birth of the
Tudor Dynasty

For Dad
You'll Never Walk Alone

Elizabeth of York and the Birth of the Tudor Dynasty

Beverley Adams

PEN & SWORD HISTORY
AN IMPRINT OF PEN & SWORD BOOKS LTD.
YORKSHIRE – PHILADELPHIA

First published in Great Britain in 2024 by
PEN AND SWORD HISTORY
An imprint of
Pen & Sword Books Ltd
Yorkshire – Philadelphia

ISBN 978 1 39904 415 8

A CIP catalogue record for this book is available from the British Library.

Typeset in Times New Roman 12/16 by
SJmagic DESIGN SERVICES, India.
Printed and bound in the UK by CPI Group (UK) Ltd.

Pen & Sword Books Limited incorporates the imprints of Atlas, Archaeology, Aviation, Discovery, Family History, Fiction, History, Maritime, Military, Military Classics, Politics, Select, Transport, True Crime, Air World, Frontline Publishing, Leo Cooper, Remember When, Seaforth Publishing, The Praetorian Press, Wharncliffe Local History, Wharncliffe Transport, Wharncliffe True Crime and White Owl.

For a complete list of Pen & Sword titles please contact
PEN & SWORD BOOKS LIMITED
George House, Units 12 & 13, Beevor Street, Off Pontefract Road,
Barnsley, South Yorkshire, S71 1HN, England
E-mail: enquiries@pen-and-sword.co.uk
Website: www.pen-and-sword.co.uk

or

PEN AND SWORD BOOKS
1950 Lawrence Rd, Havertown, PA 19083, USA
E-mail: uspen-and-sword@casematepublishers.com
Website: www.penandswordbooks.com

MIX
Paper | Supporting responsible forestry
FSC www.fsc.org FSC® C013604

Contents

Acknowledgements vii
List of Illustrations viii
Timeline of Events x
Introduction xiii
Author's Note on the Wars of the Roses 1377–1461 xvii

Chapter One	A Clandestine Marriage	1
Chapter Two	The Birth of a Princess of York	6
Chapter Three	The Royal Nursery and the Beginnings of Trouble	17
Chapter Four	Exile, War and Glory, a Princess in Sanctuary	24
Chapter Five	The Glorious Court of England	33
Chapter Six	The Downfall of Uncle Clarence	41
Chapter Seven	A Jilted Bride	49
Chapter Eight	The Fall of the House of York	53
Chapter Nine	The Rise of the House of Tudor	69
Chapter Ten	A Bride at Last	84
Chapter Eleven	Elizabeth, the Wife	90
Chapter Twelve	Elizabeth, the Mother	95
Chapter Thirteen	Elizabeth, the Queen	106
Chapter Fourteen	A Second Pretender Threatens	114
Chapter Fifteen	Victory Again	123
Chapter Sixteen	A Spanish Marriage	131
Chapter Seventeen	Death Strikes the House of Tudor	138

Appendix One The Battles of the Wars of the Roses 145
Appendix Two The Children of King Edward IV and Queen Elizabeth 146
Appendix Three *Titulus Regis* 149
Appendix Four The Annulment of the *Titulus Regis* by Henry VII 156
Appendix Five *Ordinances of a Royal Birth* by Lady Margaret Beaufort 158
Appendix Six *The Song of Lady Bessy* 160
Bibliography 165
Index 167

Acknowledgements

Many thanks as always to all at my publisher Pen & Sword for all the hard work that went into producing this book, especially Jonathan Wright for allowing me the opportunity to write this book and to Laura Hirst for all her past and future hard work she has put into getting my manuscripts 'book ready'.

As always, thanks to Mum, Dad, Chris, Paul and Alison. To Mary, Danni and Luke with a special mention to Faith, Kai and Kali. To my wonderful and supportive friends Lorraine Mawdsley, Marie Drelincourt, Elaine Drelincourt, Kathryn Baxendale, Leona Steele, Chris Smith, Gill Parker, Pat Palmer and Amy Ball. With a particular thanks to Carol Worster who, as always, is my go-to Ricardian expert. Thank you Carol for answering my endless questions, for lending me books and for taking the time to talk me through what is one of England's most controversial moments in history and for providing me with photos of Sheriff Hutton. As always a special mention goes to Emma Powell who is, and always has been, the very best of friends.

Thanks to all the historians who have gone before me, to all the wonderful archivists and The Royal Collection for allowing me permission to use images held by them.

Finally, a special thank you to Elizabeth of York. A woman whose life has for so long been overshadowed by her son and grandchildren. A woman who deserved her own life to be recognised and celebrated and I am honoured to have been given that opportunity.

As a Lancastrian it was a pleasure to get to know this wonderful princess of York and Queen of England, the mother of the Tudor dynasty.

List of Illustrations

Elizabeth of York, the British School via the Royal Collection Trust © **His Majesty King Charles III 2023**.

King Edward IV, via the Royal Collection Trust © **His Majesty King Charles III 2023**.

Elizabeth Woodville, via the Royal Collection Trust © **His Majesty King Charles III 2023**.

King Henry VII, Artist Unknown, via Wiki Commons

Prince Arthur Tudor, Prince of Wales, via the Royal Collection Trust © **His Majesty King Charles III 2023**.

Princess Margaret Tudor, later Queen of Scotland, via the Royal Collection Trust © **His Majesty King Charles III 2023**.

King Henry VIII, by Hans Holbein the Younger, via Wiki Commons

Princess Mary Tudor, later Queen of France and Duchess of Suffolk, via Wiki Commons

George, Duke of Clarence, by Lucas Cornelisz de Kock, via Wiki Commons

King Richard III, via Wiki Commons

Margaret of York, Duchess of Burgundy, via Wiki Commons

Cecily Neville, Duchess of York, by Meister der Munchner Legenda Aurea, via Wiki Commons

The Princes in the Tower, by John Everett Millais, 1878, via Wiki Commons

Perkin Warbeck, the pretender, via Wiki Commons

Lambert Simnel, the pretender, via Wiki Commons

Queen Mary Tudor, granddaughter of Elizabeth of York and Henry VII, via Wiki Commons

Lady Elizabeth, later Queen Elizabeth I, granddaughter of Elizabeth of York and Henry VII via Wiki Commons

King Edward VI, via Wiki Commons

The ruins of Sheriff Hutton Castle, North Yorkshire © Carol Worster, 2023

The ruins of Middleham Castle, North Yorkshire, author's own image

The Tower of London

The Tudor Rose

The Queen of Hearts playing card supposedly based on Elizabeth of York

The tomb of King Richard III at Leicester Cathedral, author's own image

Timeline of Events

1437	Birth of Elizabeth Woodville at Grafton, Northamptonshire.
28 April 1442	Birth of Edward IV at Rouen, France to Richard, Duke of York and Cecily Neville, Duchess of York.
28 January 1457	Birth of Henry Tudor at Pembroke Castle to Margaret Beaufort and Edmund Tudor, Earl of Richmond.
2 February 1461	The Battle of Mortimer's Cross.
17 February 1461	The Second Battle of St Albans.
4 March 1461	King Edward IV is declared King of England.
29 March 1461	The Battle of Towton.
1 May 1464	Marriage between Edward IV and Elizabeth Woodville.
October 1464	The Earl of Warwick discovers the marriage between Edward IV and Elizabeth Woodville.
11 February 1466	Birth of Princess Elizabeth of York, eldest child of King Edward IV and Elizabeth Woodville at Westminster Palace.
11 August 1467	Birth of Princess Mary of York.
20 March 1469	Birth of Princess Cecily of York.
3 October 1470	King Edward IV flees England and goes into exile in Flanders, forcing his queen and children into sanctuary at Westminster Abbey.
2 November 1470	Birth of Edward, Prince of Wales, future King Edward V.

11 April 1471	King Edward returns to England and is restored to the throne.
14 April 1471	The Battle of Barnet.
4 May 1471	The Battle of Tewkesbury.
21 May 1471	Death of King Henry VI at the Tower of London.
10 April 1472	Birth of Princess Margaret of York.
17 August 1473	Birth of Prince Richard, Duke of York.
2 November 1475	Birth of Princess Anne of York.
March 1477	Birth of Prince George, Duke of Bedford (Dies March 1479).
18 February 1478	George, Duke of Clarence is executed at the Tower of London on the orders of his brother, Edward IV.
14 August 1479	Birth of Princess Catherine of York.
10 November 1480	Birth of Princess Bridget of York.
9 April 1483	Death of Edward IV aged forty at Westminster, his son becomes King Edward V.
16 March 1485	Death of Anne Neville, Queen Consort of King Richard III.
26 June 1485	Reign of King Richard III begins.
22 August 1485	Henry Tudor defeats King Richard III at the Battle of Bosworth to become King of England. Death of King Richard III.
18 January 1486	Henry VII marries Elizabeth of York.
20 September 1486	Birth of Prince Arthur Tudor.
25 November 1487	Coronation of Elizabeth of York.
28 November 1489	Birth of Princess Margaret Tudor, future Queen of Scotland.
28 June 1491	Birth of Prince Henry, future King Henry VIII.
8 June 1492	Death of Elizabeth Woodville at Bermondsey Abbey.

2 July 1492	Birth of Princess Elizabeth Tudor.
14 September 1495	Death of Princess Elizabeth Tudor.
18 March 1496	Birth of Princess Mary Tudor, future Queen of France and Duchess of Suffolk.
21 December 1499	Birth of Prince Edmund Tudor, Duke of Somerset.
19 June 1500	Death of Prince Edmund Tudor, Duke of Somerset.
14 November 1501	Prince Arthur marries Katherine of Aragon.
2 April 1502	Death of Prince Arthur.
2 February 1503	Birth of Princess Katherine Tudor, she died days following her birth.
11 February 1503	Death of Queen Elizabeth of York, aged thirty-seven at Tower of London.
21 April 1509	Death of King Henry VII, his son, Prince Henry accedes to the throne as King Henry VIII.

Introduction

When people asked me who I was writing about for my next book they would often look at me for further clarification. Elizabeth of York? Who was she? My standard response would be Elizabeth of York, she was the mother of Henry VIII. I felt like I almost had to apologise on Elizabeth behalf for not having a 'Tudor style reputation' but to be the daughter, wife, mother and grandmother of monarchs must have meant she had a story to tell.

So just who exactly was Elizabeth of York? She was the eldest child of the enigmatic Yorkist King Edward IV and his queen, Elizabeth Woodville. She was the wife and queen of King Henry VII and the mother of King Henry VIII, Queen Margaret of Scotland and Queen Mary of France making her the grandmother of King Edward VI, Queen Mary I, Queen Elizabeth I and King James V of Scotland. She is often described as being the ideal role model of what a queen in the late medieval and early Tudor period ought to have been. Amongst many things, she was pious, kind and most importantly, fertile.

But what has this done for her reputation? We are all aware of the lives of her son and his six wives, her grandchildren and even her great-granddaughter, Lady Jane Grey, the 'nine-days queen' is better known than Elizabeth. It is not often we hear of her fiercely defending her husband's right to rule, when in fact it should have been her crown by right, or of her being a loving mother who was devastated by the death of three of her children. We never hear of all her charitable and good works; it is all overshadowed by those around her. Her husband, Henry Tudor, later Henry VII, claimed his crown after defeating Elizabeth's uncle Richard III at the Battle of Bosworth on 22 August 1485 but his claim was weak and tenuous to say the least. His right to rule came by the right of conquest but knew a marriage to Elizabeth of York would bolster his claim further given how well respected she was amongst the Yorkist faction.

There are no stories of Elizabeth passionately standing up to her husband, reports suggest she was meek and mild and did what was expected of her, she stood by her husband's side and produced heirs, that was her role and that is what she did. Thankfully, Elizabeth inherited her mother's ability to bear many children, she gave Henry two male heirs who survived early childhood, although the eldest, Prince Arthur, heir to the Tudor dynasty died at the age of 15, just six months after his marriage to Katharine of Aragon. Arthur's death signalled the need for the second son, Henry, Duke of York to step forward to take on the role of being heir to the throne. The ginger haired Henry was said to be Elizabeth's favoured child, he was loud, robust and ready to rule, and even at a young age he understood his importance in the world.

That little boy would go on to become King Henry VIII, one of England's most notorious rulers and the complete opposite in character to the mother he idolised, he inherited many of his character traits from his maternal grandfather Edward IV. Elizabeth would spend as much time as she could with her children who had been given their own household at Eltham Palace under the watchful gaze of their tutors. She would teach her daughters Margaret and Mary all they would need to know to be dutiful wives and how to run a large household but also how to be queens, tasks Elizabeth excelled in. She was a kind and patient mother who doted on her children and moulded them into monarchs that would rule at home and abroad.

But are we being fair in casting Elizabeth in this light? Is it a true reflection of her life and role as Queen? Yes, she played the role of submissive queen to perfection but that is not to say she was ineffectual in her role as consort and had no sway at court. Like any married woman she knew how to persuade her husband to hear her point of view and Henry was no different to any other man, but because much of her discussions with Henry took place in private we cannot truly gauge how effective she was in her ability to persuade him on matters of state. He did not change his mind often on state matters but he did, on numerous occasions, listen and take on board Elizabeth's point of view and considered her arguments.

The couple were close and this was a marriage based on deep affection and trust. The king valued his wife's opinion as did the many courtiers who would often approach Elizabeth to ask her to intercede with the king on their behalf. For this, she was well liked and respected, she was capable of pulling in the Yorkist faction who remained loyal to her and the memory of her father, but she also deftly navigated the Lancastrian members of court.

She was able to bridge the gap between the two warring royal households and brought about a unity the country had so longed for. She never favoured one side over the other and remained utterly neutral in court affairs, unlike her mother. She never sought to elevate one faction over another, having seen the troubles caused during the reign of her father she must have learnt favouritism could bring no happiness and peace. Elizabeth was a well measured woman who had the ability to remain calm and in control. She was adept at welcoming foreign ambassadors and gave to as many charitable causes as she could but she knew her place was not to get involved in the running of the country; politics was not the place of the queen.

But Elizabeth did court her own scandal during the reign of her uncle King Richard III when it was thought she schemed to marry him in order to become queen. She knew she was her father's legitimate heir following the suspicious deaths of her younger brothers in the Tower of London and wanted to take her rightful place as queen of England. Marriage to Henry Tudor had meant she had succeeded in doing that and once she sat securely on the throne she meekly retreated to the background and did as her husband bid. She never caused controversy once she was married and always put her husband's interests before her own. Elizabeth may have been a queen but she was also a mother and that was one area of diplomacy Henry allowed her to be involved in, the marriages of their children and as queen she would have been expected to take an active part in those discussions.

But Elizabeth was not a woman who would stand by and watch injustices being done to those in less fortunate positions, she would often intercede on behalf of her servants and would even sometimes sort matters without consulting the king first, proving she perhaps did involve herself in court matters to some degree. She was happy to help those who had been loyal to her or her family and often helped financially to support those who had fallen on hard times, even to her own financial detriment for Elizabeth was not independently wealthy.

Throughout her life Elizabeth had been over-domineered by the women surrounding her. Her mother was overpowering and involved herself in court affairs, as did her paternal grandmother Cecily Neville and her overbearing mother-in-law Margaret Beaufort who was a constant figure in her marriage. Many like to cast doubt on their relationship but there is no evidence to suggest they did not get on especially as it was Margaret who was the driving force behind her sons marriage to Elizabeth, to which Elizabeth was grateful.

Queen Elizabeth was kind, virtuous and pious and through her the Tudor dynasty was born, her son became one of England's well-known monarchs and her granddaughter England's first queen regnant, they may all be better known but without the legacy of Elizabeth of York the Tudor's may have been consigned to the footnotes of history. She was well loved by her husband and the legend is that he used Elizabeth for the very first queen of hearts playing card.

Author's Note on the Wars of the Roses 1377–1461

Written below is a brief account of a series of battles known as the Cousin's War which we now know as the Wars of the Roses that took place between the House of Lancaster and the House of York in the fourteenth and fifteenth centuries. This account covers the time from the death of King Edward III in 1377 to the accession of King Edward IV in 1461. The remainder of the story will be told throughout the book as and when the need arises, but in order to understand Elizabeth then we must understand what life was like for her ancestors and the battles that ensued which saw her take the throne as a Queen of England.

The Wars of the Roses, or the Cousin's War as it is sometimes referred to, brought bloodshed and uncertainty to the realm of England for over 100 years. On one side was the red rose House of Lancaster and on the other the white rose House of York, and it was two sides of the same family who went to war over the throne of England. The root cause of the war goes as far back as 1377 when King Edward III died leaving his 10-year-old grandson as his heir. King Richard II was the son of Edward III's eldest son Edward, Prince of Wales, otherwise commonly referred to as the Black Prince, and his wife Joan of Kent.

Sadly, Prince Edward died in June 1346 leaving his son Richard the heir to his grandfather. The reign of Richard II was far from glorious because he managed to create huge divides between the crown and the country's leading nobility. Richard's main aim was to reduce the power of his uncles and in particular that of John of Gaunt, Duke of Lancaster and when he died in in 1399, Richard exiled his son, Henry Bolingbroke, to France. When Richard went on an expedition to Ireland, Bolingbroke seized his chance to return and in June 1399 he invaded England where he met with little resistance seeing his support grow fast. Bolingbroke managed to depose Richard and was crowned King Henry IV on 13 October 1399 at Westminster Abbey making him England's first Lancastrian king. Richard was taken as prisoner to Pontefract Castle, Yorkshire where he died in February 1400, it is believed he was starved to death although there is no concrete evidence to support this and his exact cause of death remains unknown.

Henry IV's early reign was far from smooth as he faced various pockets of rebellion especially from Welsh nobles who had been one-time supporters of Richard. Their rebellion, led by Owain Glyndŵr, would in fact last longer than Henry's reign, the fight for independence did not die with him. The king died in 1413 and his son Henry was crowned as King Henry V. Again, this was a reign that suffered challenges including the 'Southampton Plot' which was led by Sir Thomas Grey, Baron Scrope and Richard of Conisbrough. Conisbrough, also Earl of Cambridge, was the second son of Edmund of Langley, Duke of York and it was his intention to replace Henry V with his uncle, Edmund Mortimer who just happened to be a great-great-grandson of Edward III via the line of Edward's second son Lionel of Antwerp. Much to Mortimer's credit he remained loyal to his king and advised him of the plot leading to the three ringleaders being arrested and executed. Conisbrough's son Richard of York would go on to inherit the Mortimer claim to the throne and the Dukedom of York following the death of the childless Edmund Duke of York, the elder brother of his father.

In October 1415 Henry V won a famous battle at Agincourt against the French and this seemed to finally secure him on his throne. He went on to marry Catherine of Valois with whom he had one child, a son called Henry. Sadly, just nine months after his birth his father died meaning the infant Henry acceded to the throne as King Henry VI.

Due to his tender years, he needed a regent to govern for him until he came of age at 16 in 1437. His mother Catherine of Valois remarried following the death of her husband and with her new husband, Owen Tudor she had two sons, Edmund and Jasper and both would become instrumental as the wars continued to their bloody end.

The Earl of Suffolk's reputation had grown at court and like Henry VI he was in favour of diplomacy over a military campaign but that put him at odds with Richard, Duke of York. Suffolk had managed to broker a peace deal with the French and part of the treaty was the marriage of Henry to Margaret of Anjou. Once again, York was outspoken in his criticism and as a result he was stripped of his post in France and sent to Ireland where he was given a tenure of ten years, it was clear people wanted him kept as far away from court as possible.

Over time it became apparent that Suffolk was the real power behind the throne but as things continued to deteriorate in France the king decided to exile him, although he was captured on his way to the coast and executed. Into his shoes stepped Edmund Beaufort, Duke of Somerset, and grandson of John of Gaunt. He had taken over from York's post in France and over time he began to grow close to the queen which drew widespread criticism. Queen Margaret had complete control over her hapless husband and alongside Somerset they began to rule England. Henry and Margaret struggled to conceive a child but did eventually have a son, Edward of Westminster, the Prince of Wales, in October 1453 eight years after they had married which led many to believe Somerset was the real father.

It quickly became clear that the king was suffering from some sort of mental illness as he showed a complete lack of interest in leadership and became more and more fanatical about religion and learning than he was at governing his country. In 1453, England lost hold on all her final territories in France save Calais bringing to an end the Hundred Years' War. This catastrophic news caused Henry to suffer a complete mental collapse and Richard, Duke of York was recalled from his post in Ireland to be named Lord Protector and chief councillor on 27 March 1454.

By 1455 Henry seemed to have recovered and returned to govern, he reversed much of what York had done who had once again been forced back into exile in Ireland but his supporters, mainly the Earl of Warwick and his father the Earl of Salisbury, publicly backed Richard and the House of York. The king and Somerset, along with others, decided to hold a meeting of the Great Council safely away from London in Leicester but on 22 May 1455 York gathered his supporters and marched to intercept the royal party at St Albans. York led troops numbering around 5,000 whilst the king had only around 2,000 at his back and on 22 May the Battle of St Albans took place. It proved to be a decisive victory for York and as a result they took the king prisoner, whose health once again deteriorated and York was reappointed as Lord Protector.

In retaliation the Lancastrians managed to ambush the Yorkists which forced Warwick to sail from his post in Calais back to England with troops but this turned out to be an unmitigated disaster as many of his troops defected. The battle of Ludford Bridge was a moment of victory for Lancaster, the battle took place not far from York's stronghold of Ludlow Castle, the town itself was ransacked and he fled from there with his second son Edmund, Earl of Rutland and headed for the safety of Ireland whilst his eldest son, Edward, Earl of March headed to Calais with Warwick and Salisbury. York and his sons were wanted men and by late 1460 Warwick, Salisbury and Edward sailed for England. When they arrived, Warwick and Edward chased the king north whilst Salisbury headed to London to secure the Tower.

The two forces finally came head-to-head on 10 July 1460 at Northampton where the Yorkists triumphed, once again. Henry became a prisoner of York and was sent to London and to the Tower. Later that year York and Edmund returned from Ireland, the duke attended parliament in the October and he left people in little doubt over his true intentions to claim the crown when he boldly placed his hand upon the throne. This action shocked many in attendance and even unsettled some of his allies, they were willing to support him, but only to a certain extent.

Meanwhile, queen Margaret had travelled north to Scotland to amass support, she did the same in France which meant the Auld Alliance now fully supported the Lancastrian cause. Support in the north was strong for the red rose and soon the two sides were ready to do battle again. York arrived at his northern stronghold of Sandal Castle, near Wakefield and for some unknown reason he decided to leave the safety of the castle walls on 30 December. York, his son Rutland and Warwick's younger brother Thomas Neville were captured and executed. Salisbury had managed to flee the battlefield but was captured later that night. He was taken from Pontefract Castle and was executed the day after. York's death meant his dukedom and claim to the throne now passed on to his son Edward who on 2 February 1461 trounced a Lancastrian army at Mortimer's Cross, Owen Tudor, king Henry's step-father was captured and executed at Hereford. The next meeting between the two sides was to be on 17 February in what has become known as the Second Battle of St Albans. It was a battle won by the Lancastrians and once again Henry was restored to his throne.

Warwick marched his troops to meet Edwards and together they marched on London, knowing the Lancastrians were not popular in the capital, the queen and her men had even been refused entry so they knew they had to seize the moment. Edward was proclaimed king as King Edward IV of England and he was everything Henry was not. He stood tall at 6ft 4", he was strong, athletic, brave and young but in order to cement his place on the throne he had to see off the Lancastrian cause once and for all.

He and Warwick, who later became known as the 'Kingmaker', marched out of London and headed north where they met the enemy at Towton in Yorkshire on 29 March 1461. What ensued has been described as the bloodiest battle to have ever taken place on English soil. There were approximately 50,000 men on the snowy battlefield, it lasted ten hours and despite being outnumbered the Yorkists claimed a vital victory. Henry, Margaret and their son fled to Scotland where they were later joined by their supporters, the king was captured a year later and taken back to the Tower of London. Meanwhile Edward rode to London in triumph and was crowned King of England on 28 June 1461 at Westminster Abbey, his reign would go untested until 1470.

Although this is by no means a thorough account of the Wars of the Roses what I hope it gives is some kind of perspective of what brought Edward IV to the throne. We will pick up the story of Elizabeth of York's life with the meeting of her parents. Edward had been on the throne for three years when one day he came across a beautiful woman at the side of the road…….

Chapter One

A Clandestine Marriage

On a spring day in 1464 a beautiful woman, aged about twenty-seven stood with her two young sons, Thomas and Richard, under an oak tree at the side of a country lane in the English county of Northamptonshire. As she waited patiently a handsome man in his early twenties rode past her on his fine horse but this was no chance meeting. The young woman was Elizabeth Grey (nee Woodville), a commoner and the widow of Sir John Grey, a soldier killed at the Second Battle of St Albans whilst fighting for the Lancastrian cause.

The young man on the horse was King Edward IV, the triumphant Yorkist king. As the king rode by where Elizabeth was standing she is said to have caught his eye, he was said to have been captured by her beauty and in that moment he wished her to be his mistress. Elizabeth declined, all she wanted from the king was the reinstatement of her deceased husband's properties that her mother-in-law had removed from her following his death, she saw them as her son's rightful inheritance and after a failed attempt to enlist the support of the Lord Chamberlain, Lord Hastings, she saw petitioning the king directly as the only option left to her. But the king was a persistent man and as king often got what he wanted and he wanted Elizabeth Grey.

The couple were secretly married on May Day 1464 at her parents' home at Grafton in a small chapel within the estate's grounds. Joining the bride and groom were Elizabeth's mother, Jacquetta of Luxembourg, two other gentle women, the priest and the priest's assistant. To account for his absence, the king gave the excuse to his men that he was going out hunting, he also told Elizabeth's father, Baron Rivers, that he would be enjoying his hospitality for a few days. When in residence at Grafton the king arranged for Elizabeth to be brought to his rooms in secret, here the newlyweds could be alone, safe in the knowledge that her mother was keeping the whole affair a secret from the family. Not only did she become Edward's wife that day, she also became Queen of England.

Whether this account of the meeting of Elizabeth and Edward IV is true is not known but this is the romanticised version of how Elizabeth of York's parents met and made one of English royal history's most controversial marriages.

The marriage was kept a secret for many months because they both knew it would be an unpopular choice amongst Edward's nobles as she was so far beneath him in status. But to them the most unforgivable and unfathomable reason would be that by marrying an English commoner the king had removed any prospect of a lucrative foreign marriage. A foreign match would have brought wealth and prosperity to the country but more importantly an alliance with one of Europe's powerhouses would have been hugely beneficial in terms of peace and trade and they are often brought about by marriage. England was fragile following the Cousin's War and whilst Edward sat upon his throne the Lancastrian king, Henry VI, still lived in the Tower of London. Henry may have been Edward's prisoner but his very being could cause an uprising at any moment. So, he stalled telling his council of his marital status meaning Elizabeth began to worry he would pass her over or that he could be talked out of the marriage for a better offer. After all, she was older than him, a widow with two sons and poor, meaning there was no dowry, something a European royal bride would have brought in abundance.

They could not stall for much longer; Edward knew he would have to break the news sooner or later, he could protect Elizabeth to some extent but he would have to stand in front of the council and confess to them he had made a marriage that benefitted the state in no way – he had married for love. In September 1464, he stood before the council at Reading Abbey and told the men gathered in front of him that he had married without their guidance. Needless to say, they were apoplectic with rage. Many were shocked he had gone against the express wishes of his own advisors, the rest were just simply furious. The angriest amongst them was Richard Neville, the Earl of Warwick, he had been given the moniker of the 'King-Maker' given his role in securing Edward on his throne. He had invested a lot of time in working to bring about a marriage with either Bona of Savoy who was the daughter of the Duke of Savoy or Isabella of Castille (she would go on to marry Ferdinand of Aragon and their daughter Katherine would marry Elizabeth of York's sons, firstly Prince Arthur and then King Henry VIII). Edward's rejection of Bona of Savoy would have later implications when she refused to consider a marriage between the king's son and her daughter, she obviously felt slighted by the fact she had been overlooked for a commoner but would later go on to marry the Duke of Milan.

Warwick felt the king had been stupid, he could not believe he had made such a political mistake, it is not as though he was new to the throne because he had been ruling for three years and should have known kings did not marry for love and that it was their duty to marry where it best suited their country. Warwick was going to have to work hard to rebuild the bridges Edward had so thoughtlessly broken down, there was no hiding from the fact that this marriage had huge political ramifications that would be felt throughout Edward's tenure as king.

As the news broke, Elizabeth and her family were summoned from Grafton, to join the king at Reading where she was formally introduced to the council as queen on 29 September 1464. She was escorted by Warwick and the Duke of Clarence, Edward's younger brother, into the Abbey. Many were shocked by the news and felt Elizabeth must have used some form of witchcraft against the king in order to ensnare him, but regardless of what they thought, she was now their queen and her large family were on the rise, much to the disdain of the established nobility. The Woodvilles are often cast as the lowly commoners who took advantage where they could but that is not strictly true. Elizabeth's mother was Jacquetta of Luxembourg, she was the daughter of Peter the I of Luxembourg, Count of Saint-Pol, Conversano and Brienne and Margaret of Baux. Jacquetta's first marriage was to John of Lancaster, Duke of Bedford, he was the third son of King Henry IV. Jacquetta was only 17 years old when she married for the first time, the ceremony took place on 20 April 1433 in Thérouanne, Northern France and was officiated by her uncle in his role as bishop. Sadly, the couple were only married for just over two years as John died in Rouen on 14 September 1435. As the Duchess of Bedford, a title she was permitted to keep even following her second marriage, Jacquetta travelled to England, her escort, as appointed by Henry VI, was Sir Richard Woodville and during that trip the couple fell in love.

They married in secret in early 1437 and did so without permission of the king and when he heard the news he was upset and declined them an audience. He fined the couple £1000 (approximately £640,000 today) and upon payment he welcomed them back to court where they enjoyed a favoured position. Jacquetta was a very powerful lady; she was related to both the king and the queen through marriage making her the most senior lady at court after queen Margaret of Anjou. Their popularity was cemented when King Henry created Richard Baron Rivers in 1448 and they were firm supporters of the House of Lancaster which meant when their daughter married the Yorkist King their allegiance had to change with it. The marriage was a very happy one and produced fourteen children of which Elizabeth was the eldest, thirteen would survive to adulthood and when Elizabeth became queen her siblings would be the ones to benefit the most.

Arrangements were quickly made for the marriages of her siblings, her sister Margaret married Thomas Fitzalan, Lord Maltravers, the son and heir of the Earl of Arundel, sister Katherine was betrothed to Henry Stafford, Duke of Buckingham but the most astonishing marriage was that of her brother John, who at the age of 20, married Katherine Neville, Dowager Duchess of Norfolk, aged 65. This match was not well received as it was seen as nothing but a shameless grab for power and money by the queen's family. Warwick, the nephew of the dowager duchess, was again shocked and disgusted by the king's ability to make such unwise decisions. Elizabeth's brother Lionel was created Bishop of Salisbury and her younger brothers were given titles and honours. At the time, these marriages stood as proof of the power the queen had over her husband, the nobility were angry the Woodville's were marrying up the eligible sons and daughters of England's greatest families for themselves, it was a sign that all was not going to be plain sailing for the new king and queen.

Chapter Two

The Birth of a Princess of York

A royal birth has always been an event of great expectation, excitement and danger. The anticipation the child would be the much-desired male heir put huge pressure on the mother, not that she had any control over the gender of her child, but the birth of a prince was a cause of huge celebration for the court and country alike. So, when the queen of England entered her apartments at Westminster Palace in January 1466 to begin her lying in, the country held its breath. Birth in the medieval world was a dangerous thing, the mother was open to infection and the risk of huge blood loss was a very real danger.

No doubt the queen was well tended to with the best care on hand, her mother and other female family members would have been present to assist midwife Margaret Cobbe, the older women, or those who had given birth before would have been there to support the queen as she travailed through labour. It was also not the first time she had given birth, she had two sons from her previous marriage so knew what was ahead of her. The lying-in chamber was a strictly man-free zone, only women were allowed to enter and the room was to remain dark and hot. The windows were sealed shut, huge biblical tapestries would have adorned the walls and the fire banked up, the cradle would have been built ready for the babes arrival.

On 11 February 1466 the queen safely delivered her child, she gave birth to a daughter that would be named for her. The Princess Elizabeth of York was her father's heir and there is no evidence to suggest he was disappointed with her arrival; in fact, he presented his wife with a rather lavish jewel in celebration of their daughters safe arrival. He had much to be encouraged by after all, he was young and his wife had borne sons before so surely it was only a matter of time before his prince arrived but until that time came, Princess Elizabeth was the jewel of the court. To Edward she was the embodiment of god's approval that his marriage was sound and his reign valid and his little princess was the apple of his eye.

Following the birth, Elizabeth would have been cleaned, swaddled and placed in her cradle of state where she would be watched over by her team of rockers, nursery attendants and wet nurse. Her mother would have had little to do as it was her duty to recover from the birth as quickly as possible. In order for the queen to be able to fully rest and recuperate the young princess was given a household of her own from birth. As the heir to the throne Elizabeth's baptism was a stately affair, the king celebrated his daughter's arrival as if she had been a boy. The ceremony took place in St. Stephen's Chapel within Westminster Palace and was officiated by Warwick's brother George Neville, Archbishop of York. Her godmothers were her grandmothers, Jacquetta, Duchess of Bedford and Cecily Neville, Duchess of York with the Earl of Warwick standing as her godfather.

As was customary at the time her parents did not attend the baptism and we have very few other details of the actual ceremony available to us. The queen was still confined to her chamber and would not be able to leave it until forty days after the birth, at which point she would undergo a ceremony called churching. This was a ceremony that cleansed the queen and made it possible for her to return to court, and her husbands bed.

It was a grand affair, a stately procession was headed by a selection of priests all bearing relics, scholars carrying candles, they led a group of grand ladies who were followed by musicians such as pipers and the King's Choir. Behind them came twenty-four heralds and sixty earls and knights of the realm, finally came the triumphant queen with two dukes by her side carrying the canopy of estate over her head. Despite the pomp and ceremony, the service was solemn, it was one of purification that marked her return to court life as queen and to her husband's bed, ready to conceive the desired prince. Following the service came a grand feast where the queen, who wanted to make a show of her grandeur and position, sat alone at the high table on an elaborate gold throne. Standing close by ready to assist her were her mother and sister-in-law, Anne, Duchess of Exeter. Once the first dish of food had been served and tasted by the queen the rest of her guests could take their seats, although those ladies responsible of serving the queen did so on their knees. The feasting lasted about three hours and was taken in complete silence, this all smacks of Elizabeth Woodville wanting to remind everyone she was queen, regardless of what people thought of her marriage and family she was their queen and deserved their respect and she was determined they would give it. It may be a woman attempting to assert her power but it also shows a power hungry one who looked proud and above her station. After the silent meal, there was to be music and dancing which sounds much more exciting for the guests.

As court life resumed for the king and queen the baby Princess Elizabeth started her life in the care of Margaret Berners, daughter of Sir Richard Berners and wife of John Bourchier, Constable of Windsor Castle. Margaret was in charge of the overall running of the royal nursery, she would have ensured the baby was cared for day and night and that she wanted for nothing. As was customary for the time Elizabeth would have been tightly swaddled for the first eight months of her life, this was done in order to straighten her limbs as quickly as possible.

Berners would also have overseen the Pages of the Chamber and the rockers of the cradle whose job it was to help the baby princess fall asleep, or to soothe her when she became distressed. The queen would not have fed her daughter herself; this was frowned upon amongst the nobility so a wetnurse would have been employed to feed the baby. The wetnurse would be a woman who had recently given birth and would have been chosen based on her health and wellbeing for it was an important role to have. Her parents were busy so their interaction with Elizabeth would have been minimal, but they would have been assured she was being well tended to, the appointment of Lady Berners would have been made by the queen, who no doubt scrutinised many fine ladies before deciding on the one who would take care of her very important charge. The queen would have vetted and appointed most of the nursery staff, maybe with the help of Margaret Berners but to have a role within the royal nursery was one of pride.

Whilst the infant princess slept soundly in her cradle her father's grip on the throne was decidedly shaky. The country was doing well under his rule but there was always an undercurrent of feeling that things could very quickly escalate into trouble and that came with the very nature of how he had won his throne. It had been hoped that with Edward IV on the throne the wars were over and peace could finally return to England. The Wars of the Roses, as we call it now, raged across England from the mid fifteenth century and was contested for almost thirty years but trouble between the houses of Lancaster and York had raged for much longer, they ravaged each other, red rose against white, one royal house against another all to claim the throne of England. Early on in the conflict it was the house of York that appeared to triumph, the Lancastrian king, Henry VI was removed from power and in his place came the young, athletic, promising Edward IV from the house of York. He would controversially be followed by his younger brother Richard III after the disappearance of Edward's two sons from the Tower of London as the young Edward V awaited his coronation.

But that was for the future because for now Edward was beginning to have problems with another of his brothers. Over time Edward's reign started to waiver, the Lancastrians loomed constantly over his shoulder and soon enough infighting and rebellion threatened to bring the house of York crashing down. At the time of Elizabeth's birth, the two opposing factions of court were the Woodville family of the queen and the supporters of Richard, Earl of Warwick. Amidst this inner turmoil were the king's younger brothers, George, Duke of Clarence and Richard, Duke of Gloucester (later Richard III). Together the brothers were invincible, but separately each had their own agenda which led to fall outs and ultimately death. Richard took control of the north on behalf of Edward and was popular. It was certainly a family at odds with itself and when Clarence united with Warwick in their dissatisfaction and with Henry VI still alive it meant Edward was under immense pressure to keep hold of his throne.

Trouble between Edward and Warwick started when the news of the king's marriage broke, and by 1468 tensions were at boiling point. Warwick decided the Woodvilles were just too much to handle, they were dangerous and unreliable and Edward was now openly going against his advisors wishes by marrying his younger sister Margaret to Charles the Bold, Duke of Burgundy, Warwick's sworn enemy. Despite Warwick's dissatisfaction Edward admired the Burgundians and aimed to align himself with their style and customs.

He admired them so much that he decided to base his court on theirs and that meant creating a court that was excessive, magnificent and grand. But for Warwick, he would have preferred a French alliance because it would then have meant France and England could unite against the Burgundians but it would appear the Woodville family were the ones pushing for the Burgundian alliance. Was this a tactic of theirs to cause more strife between Warwick and the king? From his point of view, they had no business meddling in state affairs and before long he found himself becoming more and more isolated at court. The Earl of Warwick was a powerful man with many supporters and the Woodvilles had finally pushed him too far and so he decided to take drastic action.

He turned to the king's younger brother, George, Duke of Clarence in a bid to rid the monarchy of the Woodvilles and in turn dethrone Edward. Clarence had long coveted the throne for himself, he felt it was his by right given the scandalous rumours that went around that claimed Edward was in fact a bastard. Their mother Cecily, Duchess of York stood accused of conducting an affair whilst stationed in Rouen, France with her husband the duke in 1442. The rumour was she had liaisons with an English archer named Blaybourne whilst her husband was away fighting, the result of that union was said to be Edward but it is clear that Richard, Duke of York had no doubts that he was his child and declared Edward his son and heir. There is no concrete evidence to support this theory either way; it may simply have been that Edward had been born slightly earlier than expected.

It is unlikely the duke would have accepted the baby as his own if he doubted his parentage, he would not have allowed him to take the title of Earl of March if he thought otherwise. We must bear in mind too that these rumours had not surfaced until Warwick and Clarence started to spread them which seems a pretty low blow from Clarence, it is one thing to attack your brother but a whole other to call into question your mother's virtue and credibility. It was crucial that if Clarence wanted the crown then it was imperative he got people to believe in the slanderous rumour, for if they did then that made him the rightful king.

The young duke, aged 20 at the time, was described as being tall and fair, that could be taken to mean fair as in handsome or fair as in blonde, his bearing was regal which made him look every inch a king, but the problem was, he wasn't the king and that galled him. He has never been cast as a popular figure in history and his personality is described as being weak-willed, cruel and jealous, he wanted his brother's throne and it would appear he would stop at nothing to get it. But what was the plan? Was Warwick the driving force behind this plot or did it stem from Clarence himself? It appears both men wanted the same thing and resolved to help each other get it. Warwick's position needed to be secured should Edward fall from power. He had been so instrumental in putting Edward on the throne, he had been by his side on the battle field and at court and his position of power was not one he would be willing to give up, he needed to somehow wield power through Clarence.

So, Warwick suggested to Clarence that he marry his eldest daughter Isabel and in turn overthrow Edward and place themselves on the throne. This is a clever move on Warwick's part because it ensures he had a continuous grip on power. Isabel Neville, along with her younger sister Anne, were the most coveted heiresses in the country because they stood to inherit vast lands and wealth. Clarence approached his brother and stated his interest in marrying Isabel but Edward point blank refused to even discuss the possibility. It is understandable why the king was so against the match. Warwick was already a powerful man and if his daughter married into the royal family it would increase the risk that he would become even more so. There was also the risk that if Isabel gave birth to a son then his daughters would be under threat so he remained adamant the marriage should not go ahead. As Clarence and Isabel were cousins they would need a papal dispensation before the marriage could take place. Warwick persistently pestered Edward and even though he blocked their application the necessary documents arrived dated 14 March 1469.

Sick of Edward's refusals Isabel and Clarence travelled to Calais with Warwick from Sandwich in Kent and married without the king's consent on 11 July 1469. Whilst it was not considered a treasonable offence to defy the king in this way in the fifteenth-century it would not have done the already fractured relationship between the two brothers any good. Warwick ensured that the marriage of his eldest daughter to the brother of the king of England was well known. In a fine wedding ceremony George Neville, Archbishop of York married his niece to the duke which was followed by five days of feasting and celebrating. This was seen as a declaration of war; the starting pistol had been fired and the outright flouting of the king's authority put Warwick and Clarence in direct rebellion against the monarch. In England, Robin of Redesdale had denounced the government of King Edward, Warwick and Clarence came out in support of this and the die was cast.

After the wedding celebrations were over they returned to England and began mustering their troops. The Neville family had ruled the north of England for centuries, slowly building up power bases in the County of Durham and North Yorkshire including Middleham Castle and Sheriff Hutton. Their wealth was far beyond that of their neighbours, maybe matched only by their rivals the equally powerful Percy family of Northumberland. They helped to protect England from Scottish interference and when the call to arms came the loyal troops from the north marched south, somehow managing to by-pass

Edward on the way. The king seemed to be at odds with what to do. He was angry with his brother for disobeying his orders but he clearly did not want to go into battle against him and Warwick had been a father figure to him and had done so much for him both before he was king and since. The uncharacteristic dithering meant that he dallied over the best course of action to take but he waited too long giving his opponents the opportunity to gather their forces. Warwick could already call on a vast army and with the northern troops now amalgamating with them it created a huge army, Edward would have to act and quickly.

The king mustered his troops at the Yorkist stronghold of Fotheringhay Castle in Northamptonshire, the queen and their two eldest daughters Elizabeth and Mary followed him there in June but as Edward headed north to Newark to collect more troops, the queen and her daughters went to Norwich where they were welcomed on 18 July with pageants and displays which would have no doubt delighted the young princesses. Elizabeth was just three years old at the time and it is unlikely she was told the full extent of what was happening but she more than likely picked up on her mother's distress.

When Edward arrived at Newark he heard that Redesdale's army was much larger than he had anticipated so he turned back and headed for Nottingham where he waited for further reinforcements. He had received news that Warwick and Clarence were mustering troops against him which left him in utter disbelief, it was at this point he decided to summon them both to appear before him giving them an opportunity to debunk the rumours and plead their loyalty to him. They both refused the summons and as the reality of the situation dawned on the king he struggled with what to do next. His delay allowed the two opposing forces to by-pass him in Nottingham and to rejoin to make one large force.

The royal forces were led by the Earls of Devon and Pembroke and crunch time came on 24 July 1469 at Edgecote Moor in Northamptonshire. The night before the battle Pembroke and Devon had a disagreement and decided to divide their troops which left one side of the king's army without the vital support of the archers.

During the battle there appeared to be some confusion amongst the royal army and when Warwick arrived with his elite troops panic set in. Around several thousand men fled the battlefield and that included the earl of Devon. Pembroke's men broke ranks and before long the rebels were on top. When the approaching king's own army heard of what was happening, they too broke ranks and fled in panic. It was a complete disaster for the king's men but a triumph for Warwick and his men, the king was taken prisoner and sent to Warwick Castle but was later moved to Warwick's northern stronghold at Middleham Castle in Yorkshire. Devon did not manage to get far and along with Pembroke he was captured and executed in the aftermath of the battle.

On 12 August 1469 Warwick arranged for the executions of Earl Rivers and John Woodville at Kenilworth. They stood accused of treason but how that could have been is unfathomable seeing as they were fighting on the side of their anointed king, this made the charge and trial illegal and nothing short of murder but Warwick did not care. As father and brother to the queen, this was a revenge he enjoyed carrying out, he saw it as his duty to remove those who he saw as enemies of the state. The queen's mother Jacquetta was also arrested on trumped up charges of witchcraft. She was accused of using her powers to bring about the marriage between her daughter and the king, of course there was no evidence and she was later released but all this just showed how hated the Woodville family were.

The news of these deaths reached the queen as she stayed in Norwich. Devastated by the loss of her father and brother it must have been a terrifying time for the queen and her young daughters and with Edward in captivity they had no protectors and were vulnerable to attack. As they awaited further news the queen and Elizabeth went to pray in the Lady's Chapel at Norwich cathedral. The young princesses would probably not have been aware of what their uncle had done or the threat he posed to their family; they would of course have picked up on their mother's upset but would not have been told why. It was now apparent to the queen just how despised she and her family were and when Warwick declared publicly that it was his sole intention to rid the country of her and her evil family and the Woodville councillors that sat in Edward's government she knew it was time to get to safety. The royal party left Norwich and began the journey back to London where she arrived at some point before 16 August. Along with her young daughters, the queen went straight to the safety of the Tower of London and thankfully the rebels left them in peace, they would have been safely hidden away with the princesses safely protected. But it looked like the controversial marriage was going to cost Edward his throne, it had already caused so much bloodshed and loss but neither Edward or Elizabeth were willing to give up so easily.

After Edgecote, the power was handed to Warwick, but the reality was Edward was still king. Yes, Warwick had won a decisive victory but he would need the support of the council in London for his coup to be successful. As it stood England had two kings alive and in captivity, what was Warwick's next move going to be? He dithered, he held off from executing the king but with Edward alive he, or Clarence, had no actual power because it was Edward's signature and seal that was needed on official documents. There seemed very little support for the rebels cause and Warwick did not seem as popular as he first thought, the plan was just too risky for people to get behind so he was left with no other choice but to release Edward leaving him free to take up his throne once more.

There is some confusion over Edward's release, some have suggested he managed to bribe the guards with promises of money and fine gifts and the other reports say he was released with Warwick's full knowledge. Either way it was clear Warwick was not willing to execute his anointed king and with no other plans in place there was little choice left for him or Clarence, they had to conform and accept Edward as king. Upon his release Edward forgave Warwick and his brother but did little to appease the Neville family and he created more friction when he reinstated Henry Percy as Earl of Northumberland in 1470. The Neville and Percy families had been rivals for centuries and when the Percys had earlier fought on the side of the Lancastrian army they had their titles and estates confiscated and passed over to John Neville. After the reinstatement Neville was demoted to Marquess of Montagu, a real kick in the teeth for the Nevilles. With Warwick and Clarence put in their place Edward raised his army at York and marched back to London to be reunited with his wife and daughters and to regain his throne. The invasion and victory by Warwick was a warning shot to Edward, he was not as invincible as he had thought and could be removed from his throne far easier than he first realised.

Chapter Three

The Royal Nursery and the Beginnings of Trouble

Like any king what Edward needed the most was a male heir to further secure his position and when the queen announced she was pregnant again he must have felt overjoyed and relieved. On 11 August 1467 the queen had given birth to a second daughter named Mary at Windsor Castle. Less than two years later a third daughter arrived, she was named Cecily, it looked like the elusive son was not to be for the king and queen. The royal nursery was now full with three princesses who spent the majority of their time at Sheen Palace under the care of Lady Berners. Sheen had been gifted to the queen and she chose it as the principal residence for her children.

Royal children were always set up with a household of their own and their parents would not be involved in the day to day raising of their offspring. The household was often set up away from London as a precaution against the sicknesses that often ravaged the city. The air was much cleaner upstream of London so the palaces outside of the capital were often preferred over those closer to the centre of power.

This can often be misinterpreted as being unloving on behalf of the parents or that they had a complete disinterest in their offspring but in reality they did not have the time to dedicate to their upbringing, it was much better to give them their own establishment in which they could learn their manners and become accustomed to royal life. The princesses average day would begin at around 6am and when they heard the bell tolling they would rise from their comfortable warm beds and attend the chapel for mass after which they would break their fast. Lunch would be served at around 11am and the girls would eat together in the nursery, they would be served by liveried servants which helped them get used to royal service. In the afternoon they may have played together, or the younger ones may have taken a nap until the bell for evensong tolled upon which they would process back to the chapel for mass. Supper was taken at 4pm after which they could play, learn to dance or play a musical instrument, these were important skills for girls of their status as both talents were admired in young ladies of good birth. They would retire to bed at around 8pm, if they were in residence with their parents they would go to them to receive their blessing, they were taught to hold their parents in high esteem, they must obey them in all things and their word was not to be questioned or disobeyed. After kneeling for their blessing, they would return to the bed chamber to settle down to sleep, safe in the knowledge guardsman stood at their doors to protect them.

The royal children only really attended court for religious feast days or other special occasions such as a state visit from an overseas dignitary. Including the children in these visits not only got them used to being around ambassadors but it also showed foreign powers they were the heirs and that the York dynasty had staying power. When residing at court the princesses would join their mother's household and it would be here they would really learn how to behave and what was expected from them. They would learn how to dance, embroider and converse correctly by watching and learning from the great ladies of the realm. They would be finely dressed and made into miniature versions of their mother; the girls were dressed to impress even at this young age. At this stage Elizabeth was her father's heir and a potential future queen so she had to be taught all manner of things to prepare her for that role, a son may still come but prepare her they did.

Elizabeth and all her siblings would have been taught good manners, the girls would be instructed on how to sit up straight and how to stand and how to maintain a good posture as that made a person look regal and more authoritative. They would have received instructions on how to behave at table, eating was to be done quietly, politely and cleanly. They must discreetly wipe their mouths and hands after each course and never make too much noise, they were never to be rude, never look like they are bored of the company, yawning was banned and picking your nose was an absolute no. If they were seen to be displaying any of these bad habits they would be punished with a beating, royal or not, they had to learn the appropriate way to behave. They were to only speak when invited to do so and if they were asked their opinion they were to reply promptly and clearly. But it was not just the children who had to be beyond reproach. If you wanted a role in the nursery then you had to have an impeccable past, you had to be virtuous and follow the rules precisely because if you broke them or disobeyed them you would be instantly dismissed. The king set out strict rules on how his children were to be raised and treated and he demanded these rules to be followed to the absolute letter.

The girls would have undergone some form of education when they were old enough. Elizabeth would have been taught from an early age the importance of religion and would have been taught to read her Book of Psalms from about the age of 4 years old and would have attended mass every day. The main reason for educating girls was to prepare them for life as a wife, in the case of the York princesses they would have been expected to make very good marriages and their father would try to negotiate the best marriage alliance that would suit the country's needs, royal women married to better the country's fortunes and not necessarily for love, that was a bonus.

The exception to this would be Edward and Elizabeth's youngest daughter Bridget who had been given to the church from birth, she would be raised to live her life as a nun and would enter holy orders when the time was right. It was not unusual for noble families to have one child enter into a life serving God, usually a younger son would become a priest or a daughter an abbess. Marriages of the nobility were often discussed at length with each side wanting the best deal they could get. Edward would have needed to ensure his daughters would be well looked if she should be widowed, they would be at the mercy of a foreign power so the safety and security of his child would be a major factor in deciding who he should align with. Bearing this in mind he would have to negotiate terms with a country that had a stable monarchy, he would not consider a country that was under threat, in bad financial position or if there were any health concerns with the potential suitor. Basically, he was negotiating a contract between England and a foreign alliance that he thought would bring his own country the best deal, whether that be an alliance against another foreign power should war occur or one which would benefit him financially. This was politics and not about ensuring the marital happiness of his daughter, her being in love was not something that really mattered when the deal was being struck but Edward appears to have been a loving and caring father who indulged his children so it is unlikely he would have forced his children to marry if they had strong objections to the match, but they were taught to do their duty to their father and their country.

Once a woman was married all her property and wealth automatically became her husband's for him to do with as he wished so Edward had to be careful who he negotiated with. When Elizabeth was just 20 months old he granted her the manor of Great Linford in Buckinghamshire, by doing this meant she would receive the rents from that land, it also gave her something to bring to the marriage table along with the dowry the king would provide. Arranging a marriage like this was like putting a package deal together that would be attractive and lucrative to both sides. But there was no doubt the York princesses, and Elizabeth in particular, were a very attractive option.

Elizabeth was just 4 years old when Edward officially declared her is heir apparent, this was a clear sign to Warwick, Clarence and to anyone else who dared to question his rule. It was unusual for a king to name his daughter as heir, England had never had a queen regnant before despite the attempts of Matilda in the twelfth-century to succeed her father Henry I. It would take until 1553 when Mary Tudor, Edward's great-granddaughter, became England's first queen to rule in her own right. Maybe Edward was hopeful sons would follow his three daughters but in the meantime Elizabeth was the heir to the throne of England and with that her status rose. From Clarence's point of view, he would have been hoping his brother would never have sons and that he would change his mind when it came to naming his daughter as heir. Edward could merely have been using Elizabeth as a means of showing people he had his heir, regardless of her sex but when the time came he would have faced strong opposition from his council and lords against naming a female as his heir, especially as there were male counterparts ready to take her place.

Women were not seen as competent rulers, they were viewed as being weak and too emotional to wield power effectively, in Clarence's eyes he was the rightful heir and Elizabeth would face some serious opposition if she tried to take the throne should her father die without male issue. However, if Elizabeth was married then that was a different story, with a man beside her to help her rule was an entirely different prospect and Edward knew that. So, he decided to betroth his eldest daughter and heir to the 3-year-old son of the Earl of Northumberland (later created Marquess of Montagu) John Neville. Little George was considered to be one of the country's greatest heirs but unfortunately due to his father and uncle Warwick, he ended up inheriting next to nothing.

In 1470 Edward created him the Duke of Bedford in order to raise his status to marry his daughter, when his father and uncle rebelled against the king, George lost most of his inheritance and when he came of age in 1478 his title of duke was revoked by an act of parliament due to his lack of financial funds that meant he could not maintain the life and style of a noble of that rank. The title of duke of Bedford would later be conferred on one of Edward's sons.

By the end of 1469 Edward had forgiven Warwick and Clarence and they made their return to court, much to the disgust of the queen and her family. Elizabeth had not forgotten and would never forgive them for what they did to her father and brother and if they thought she could be placated they were wrong it would be a grudge that would last. Edward never really trusted them again but he knew he needed to keep them onside because they were powerful, especially Warwick given his strength in the field, which Edward was about to learn. He had been alerted to trouble in Lincolnshire, reports were being received at court that Sir Robert Welles had attacked Gainsborough Old Hall, the home of the king's Master of the Horse Sir Thomas Burgh. Many believed this was orchestrated by Warwick in an attempt to lure Edward north and into battle but at this point the king seemed to be unaware of any plot against him. Edward turned to his old ally for help and requested the earl raise his troops to help put down this latest rebellion which he agreed to. They set off north and met the rebel army at Losecote Field in Rutland, it was only then that Edward learnt he had been lured into a trap. Robert Welles's forces had turned over to Warwick and together they were to fight the royal troops.

Warwick and Clarence were prepared to face Edward on the battlefield to win the throne but they had learnt their lessons from last time and were not going to just capture him, it was their intention to kill the king. There would be no mistakes this time but unfortunately for Warwick and Clarence, Edward too had also learnt his lesson and was better prepared to fight. The battle, which became known as the Lincolnshire Rebellion, took place on 12 March 1470 and the king's forces won the day. It was a fairly quick battle and nearly 30,000 rebels were soundly beaten and many fled the field in fear of the retribution they would face if captured.

Folklore has it that the rebels were wearing the livery of Warwick and Clarence but they threw off their coats in the hope they would not be recognised, earning the battle the name of Losecote, or Losecoat. Warwick and Clarence fled the field and headed to the coast via Kent from there they made their escape to France where King Louis XI, known as 'the universal spider' welcomed them. The French king would become instrumental in engineering a reconciliation between Warwick and his one-time enemy Margaret of Anjou, the exiled queen of the imprisoned Henry VI. Back in England, Edward's patience had finally run out, there would be no pardons this time and he had his one-time ally and brother declared traitors. The rebellions had left life in England on a knife edge and Princess Elizabeth and her sisters were about to have their protected and comfortable lives turned upside down once more. We can only guess as to what the young Princess Elizabeth's thoughts were at this time but she would have been protected somewhat against rumours against her uncle.

Chapter Four

Exile, War and Glory, a Princess in Sanctuary

As Edward and the royal family continued to assert their power, Warwick and Clarence were in France plotting their destruction. It was whilst there Warwick betrothed his youngest daughter Anne to Edward of Westminster, the son and heir of Henry VI. Margaret of Anjou was not overly thrilled by this union and only relented after King Louis applied pressure and urged her to accept Warwick's terms.

This was a very clever and shrewd move by Warwick, not only did the marriage consolidate his links with Margaret but he is clearly hedging his bets because if the plan to put Clarence and Isabel on the throne failed and it reverted to the Lancastrians then his second daughter would then be queen. Either way he was determined to rule through one of them. Clarence was under the impression the outcome of this rebellion was to put him upon what he believed was his rightful throne and whilst Warwick gave the outward appearance of adhering to that plan, in reality he was looking to restore Henry with a view of Edward and Anne becoming king and queen. The latter plan must surely have been the one that was being aimed for because from Margaret's point of view, she was expecting her son to return to England and claim his rightful throne as the heir to the House of Lancaster.

There had been reports that King Edward was looking to marry Princess Elizabeth to the young prince in the hope of uniting the two houses and thereby ending the wars. He had apparently written to Margaret suggesting the match but there is no further evidence to support this and given that the princess was at the time betrothed to George Neville the match was unlikely. Alarm bells ought to have been ringing for the duke and duchess of Clarence, how they envisaged claiming the throne whilst Margaret and her son were part of the plot clearly meant their chances were diminished.

Nevertheless, Clarence stuck with the plan Warwick had set, which was they were going to invade England with the help of Margaret of Anjou with the view of restoring the Lancastrians back on the throne. They sailed to England separately and docked at Plymouth and Dartmouth on 13 September 1470, from there they marched their troops on London collecting men as they went. It was their plan to free Henry VI from his imprisonment in the Tower and restore him to his throne. When the news reached Edward that Warwick had arrived, had troops at his back and had managed to convince his brother John Neville to come over to his side he felt the game was up. Needless to say, the betrothal between Elizabeth and John's son George was now over too after John had treacherously betrayed his King.

Edward had to act, but rather than face Warwick and Clarence on the battlefield he fled with his brother Richard, Duke of Gloucester to Flanders. Whilst Edward was safe abroad the queen was left to deal with the children and she needed to get them and herself into a place of safety. Princess Elizabeth went with her heavily pregnant mother, grandmother Jacquetta and two younger sisters into sanctuary at Westminster Abbey. They had been awoken from their slumber in the middle of the night, the small princesses were bundled onto a barge from the Tower of London where they had been staying for their own safety but without the king's protection they had no choice but to flee. They were rowed up the Thames to Westminster. As the eldest at 4 years old, Elizabeth must have been bewildered by what was going on, the small group of women must have been terrified as they approached the imposing bulk of Westminster Abbey the little girls clinging to their mother's skirts.

As they arrived at the confines of the Abbey they hurried to the St Peter's sanctuary building which was located in the north-west corner near the churchyard of St Margaret's Church. How difficult it must have been for them to walk past the Palace of Westminster, their home full of joyful memories from a much happier time. The queen registered herself and children as those appealing for the right of sanctuary. The sanctuary building was ordinarily used for real criminals such as felons, robbers and those in severe debt, it must have felt like all hope was gone as the queen of England walked through the chapels, had she really sunk to these desperate depths?

Luckily for them the kindly Thomas Milling, the Abbott of Westminster, welcomed them and insisted they lodge with him in his own private residence Cheneygates which stood next to the west door of the Abbey. He was a kind and courteous man who was not willing to see the queen and her children lodge beside those accused of robbery and murder. Although to be fair sanctuary was quiet at the time the queen arrived as many had fled to go looting on London's lawless streets. News of Warwick's arrival and the king's fleeing had spread which in turn led to a complete collapse of any law and order on the streets. Warwick's reputation even led the queen to request the Lord Mayor not interfere with his plans and to let him into the capital unchallenged.

In order to ensure they were kept in the manner to which they were accustomed Milling gave over his three best rooms to his illustrious royal guests and ensured they had everything they needed at their disposal to make their stay as comfortable as possible. Some of these rooms are still standing today and show the level of comfort the heavily pregnant queen would have enjoyed. Another bit of good news came when the council of Henry VI insisted they were to be protected in sanctuary, he even sent Elizabeth Greystoke, Lady Scrope, to wait on the queen as she approached the latter stages of her pregnancy, an event the young Elizabeth was not going to be able to avoid in the close confines of sanctuary.

As she was pregnant, midwife Marjory Cobb and physician Dr Dominic de Sirego were also allowed to enter sanctuary unimpeded. Sanctuary life was difficult for the queen, she had very little money and relied heavily on the goodness of others. Like the kind abbot, local butcher John Gould provided beef and mutton once a week for the royal family to enjoy, a local fishmonger did the same ensuring no meat was eaten on Fridays and feast days.

Whilst the queen waited for her new arrival in the safety of sanctuary at Westminster things were moving fast in London. Warwick and Clarence re-entered the city on 6 October and went straight to the Tower of London to restore Henry VI back on his throne, this would formally be done on 30 October when he was re-crowned at St Paul's Cathedral. Much to the queen's relief Warwick declared that she and her daughters were safe in sanctuary. He had earned himself a considerable reputation and was considered many things but a killer of women and children he was not. Although he stopped short of naming the queen specifically, instead he issued a proclamation to all his adherents that no churches or sanctuaries in London were to be breached or defiled, if they were caught doing so they would be put to death. Once the hapless King Henry had been restored he then became nothing but a puppet king for Warwick, he was in control and calling the shots.

There was great joy on 1 November 1470 at Cheneygates, when the queen gave birth to a healthy son who she named Edward, after his exiled father. The supporters of Warwick and Henry VI made no fuss over the birth, to them it was inconsequential, to the Yorkists however it meant they finally had a legitimate male heir, how disappointing that the queen's moment of triumph was overshadowed by the events taking place around her but she must have felt a surge of hope as she held her newborn son in her arms.

Prince Edward was christened at Cheneygates, his godmothers were his grandmother the Duchess of Bedford and Lady Scrope, the Abbot Thomas Milling and prior John Eastrey stood as his godfathers. Elizabeth took part in the ceremony too by carrying the chrism and placing the robe around her baby brother, he was christened in such a manner you could have excused him for being a child of no consequence at all rather than the heir to the crown. The queen knew her son would be a target for the rebels and resisted the urge to leave sanctuary, she knew it was the only safe place in

London for them and they were to stay for a further five months whilst they awaited Edward's return.

When the news reached Edward in Flanders that he finally had a son and heir it galvanised him and he started to make plans to return to England to reclaim his throne and his family. But before he could do anything he needed funds and for these he turned to his brother-in-law Charles, Duke of Burgundy. With the help of funds from the duke, Edward and his small band of men started to raise an army, gather a fleet and made plans to deal with Warwick once and for all.

Margaret of Anjou and Edward IV were both planning on arriving in England to claim the throne, only one would be successful and initially it looked like Edward was going to be on the losing end when his ship was denied permission to land. He had initially arrived at Cromer, off the coast of Norfolk on 12 March however the Earl of Oxford had raised enough troops to prevent his landing leaving Edward no choice but to sail further up the North Sea to Ravenspur off the coast of Yorkshire. The war weary people of England were not overjoyed to see his return but he declared he was there only to claim his dukedom of York. They agreed and he and his men were let ashore.

If Edward had been expecting to arrive home to a hero's welcome he would have been hugely disappointed, there was a distinct lack of support and he struggled to recruit more men to his ranks, the people just wanted peace and saw Edward as someone else to stir up trouble. It all changed though when Thomas Stanley arrived with a pledge of 3000 men after that, men flocked to his banner and they marched south to the midlands where Warwick was based. The support of Stanley was surprising especially given that he was married to Warwick's younger sister Eleanor and it would not be the last time he proved to be influential as he entered the battlefield.

In a surprising turn of events, Clarence grew agitated and irked by Warwick's decision to reinstate the Lancastrian king, so, he raised over 4000 men and went to join his brother. Things were looking positive for Edward and he managed to get word to the queen that he was back in England and preparing to face and put down his enemies once and for all. Warwick refused to meet Edward's forces in battle so instead he marched down to London where he arrived on 11 April, he recaptured the ailing King Henry and sent him back to the Tower. Much to his delight Edward was well received back in his capital and was re-crowned but the most pressing thing on his mind was his family, he went straight to Westminster Abbey for a service of thanksgiving after which he returned to the palace where he was reunited with his young family, he met his son and heir for the first time and embraced his precious daughters, no doubt Elizabeth was delighted to have her father back.

They all left Westminster together and went straight to Baynard's Castle, the home of Edward's mother Cecily, dowager duchess of York, where they rested and enjoyed some freedom before moving to the Tower of London for safety. The queen and her children were accompanied there by her mother and mother-in-law her brother Earl Rivers and the Archbishop of Canterbury whilst Edward went to prepare himself for battle. The threat of Margaret of Anjou loomed large and he knew he would have to face her and Warwick on the battlefield if his throne was going to finally be secure.

On Easter Sunday 13 April 1471 King Edward IV left London with his army at his back to meet the Lancastrian forces just outside Barnet. The conditions for fighting were not ideal, there was a thick fog meaning visibility was poor which in turn led to confusion in the Lancastrian ranks when they started to attack each other. Warwick saw the utter confusion at the heart of his army so decided to turn and flee the battlefield. He was not successful and was brought off his horse and killed, his brother Montagu was also slain that day. Margaret of Anjou was too late to have any effect on the battle but Edward and his men chased her across the country, he finally caught up with her at Tewkesbury before she could join with the Lancastrian forces in Wales. On 4 May the two armies met.

The battle of Tewkesbury turned out to be another Lancastrian disaster. Prince Edward of Westminster, son and heir to Henry VI was killed after the battle and Margaret of Anjou captured and taken prisoner.

The Lancastrian claim was finally over, Edward had secured his throne once and for all. The king must have left the battlefield thinking his throne was finally safe, but there was to be one more attack to deal with.

Thomas Neville, or The Bastard of Fauconberg as he was known, was cousin to Warwick and he had been ordered to raise the men of Kent and march on London. As Admiral of the Fleet, he was to sail ships up the Thames but when he requested permission to enter London, his request was denied. He told the Mayor that he had come on the orders of Warwick to remove Edward from the throne and see that Henry replaced him. Much to his disbelief he was told Warwick was dead. He forged on regardless and began to batter at the gates that had been shut in his face.

The London authorities managed to get word out urging Edward to come to London as quickly as possible as the safety of the queen, his prince and princesses was in grave danger. Fauconberg and his men laid siege to London Bridge, with their cannon aimed at that and the city but he had underestimated how hard the Londoners would fight to defend their city. Earl Rivers and the Lieutenant of the Tower aimed the tower cannons back at the enemy in defence of their city and its citizens. The Earl of Kent joined them as they also raised the garrison of 500 men and led them out onto the streets of London to help fight the men Fauconberg had sent directly to the Tower. Inside the Tower Elizabeth must have heard and maybe seen the fighting in the streets below, it must have been a terrifying ordeal for her after spending five months in sanctuary they were now faced with the booming noise of cannon fire. Knowing it was a lost cause Fauconberg retreated back to Stratford and boarded his ships where he crossed back over the river into Kent. He aborted any further plans to capture Edward when he heard of his cousin's death and the fall of the Lancastrian cause. Fauconberg was eventually captured and sent to Middleham Castle where he was executed on 22 September 1471, his head was sent back to London where it was impaled on London Bridge, looking towards Kent.

On 21 May, King Edward arrived back in London to rapturous applause, there were trumpets and banners strewn across the city.

the war was over, for now, and the 5-year-old Elizabeth must have finally felt a sense of security now her father was back on his throne. Her time in sanctuary and the time she spent in the Tower of London under siege will have been a harrowing time for her. She witnessed the heartbreak of her mother, having to watch her cry and wail at the family's misfortune, the birth of prince Edward being the only positive light amongst months of darkness and uncertainty. But now she was back home in her palaces with fresh air in her lungs and the freedom to play with her sisters, the family was reunited at last but there was still work to be done.

Whilst Edward had won the battles and sat safely on his throne there was always going to be a threat whilst Henry VI lived. He remained a focal point for any Lancastrian rebellion and it would be an endless stream of battles that Edward would have to face if the old king lived. The same night Edward made his triumphant return to London, Henry VI was murdered in his rooms at the Tower, an order that many historians agree was given by Edward himself. The official word from the crown was that he had died of melancholy following the death of his son and heir and the acceptance that his crown was lost forever. However, the rumours that circulated were that he was struck on the back of the head whilst kneeling at prayer sometime between 10 and 11 o'clock that night.

Whilst King Edward was the man to give the order many thought it was the work of his youngest brother, Richard, Duke of Gloucester, people believed it was him that threw the fatal blow as he was supposedly staying at the Tower that night. Or did Edward ask Clarence to murder the former king in a show of loyalty towards him? Sadly, it is something we will never know for certain. Henry VI lay in St Paul's Cathedral so people could see him and know he really was dead, from there he was taken to Chertsey Abbey for burial (his remains were later reinterred by King Richard III at St Georges Chapel, Windsor) King Henry VI was king for just short of fifty years. It was a troubled reign from the start and he was often seen as a weak and incapable ruler, he suffered from periods of ill health that allowed others to exploit his vulnerabilities. His reign is not often talked about for its achievements rather than for its failures both in France and at home in England. But it would be remiss of me not to mention the legacies that he did leave behind including the founding of Eton College, King's College, Cambridge and All Souls College, Oxford. He was a pious man of great learning and his love of education has left a lasting impression on England today.

Now that Edward was safe and secure on his throne, with his son and heir now born he could turn to the role of kingship, England was now his and finally he could rule the country how he wished, safe in the knowledge that the threats had been dealt with. But, medieval England was a brutal place, especially when you have a throne to defend and there was one more challenge for Edward to overcome. This time it would be his troublesome brother George, Duke of Clarence, he lingered in the background, with Edward never knowing if he could be fully trusted and it came down to their mother to act as a mediator between the two. Clarence was given a reprieve but Queen Elizabeth still harboured anger and wanted revenge for the execution of her father and brother. She was a woman who had suffered greatly thanks to his rebellious deals with Warwick and one day she would show her hand and make him pay the ultimate price.

Chapter Five

The Glorious Court of England

Edward had a vision of how he wanted his court to look and behave and in 1472 the so-called *The Black Book* was written by members of Edward's court and from this the rules of the English court and etiquette were taken. It was heavily influenced by the Burgundian court which focussed on creating a show of magnificence and regal grandeur. The projection of majesty had now become more important than ever, Edward needed to show his court and his people that he was king and that there were no other pretenders left to challenge him. The court was to be split into two separate 'houses'. Firstly, the Lord Chamberlain's department which became known rather grandly as 'The King's House of Magnificence' and the Lord Steward's department known as 'The House of Providence'. The point of this was to create a spectacle for visitors, the walls were hung with the richest of tapestries, the furniture was the best money could buy and the king himself, and no doubt his family too, were adorned in the finest of fabrics and the costliest of jewels. Many commented how grand the court of Edward IV was, the glittering court of England was finally emerging after the dark years of war and it was here that Princess Elizabeth and her siblings grew up.

From a young age, Elizabeth would have been taught of her importance, her royal personage and how to behave in public. She would have been taught to be proud of her Plantagenet roots but also that her Woodville ones were nothing to be ashamed of, despite what people may say of her mother and her relations. Elizabeth was said to resemble her father in many ways, both were said to have a cheerful and friendly disposition although if riled they could have a temper on them and both enjoyed the finer things that life had to offer. Father and daughter enjoyed good food and luxurious clothes and both enjoyed all the courtly revels, I imagine Elizabeth was thrilled when her father introduced his new rules for decadence and finery. But as a young Princess, Elizabeth was taught to be polite and beyond reproach, she was a kind and loving child, she revered her parents, loved her siblings and was devoted to her religious studies and to God. Even though the arrival of Prince Edward altered her status, she was still the king's eldest daughter which made her a prized possession in the marriage market and Edward would hope to make sure she married well. Out of all the jewels that sparkled at the new court of King Edward IV, none shone brighter than his eldest daughter, the princess Elizabeth.

The York children would have spent some of their childhood at the Palace of Placentia in Greenwich (sometimes known as Greenwich Palace) on the south bank of the River Thames. It was surrounded by plenty of green fields and in 1485 Elizabeth's father donated some of the land to the Observant Friars who established a friary, the church would prove to be a popular choice for royal baptisms and wedding ceremonies in the years during and following Elizabeth's time as queen.

It was not uncommon for royal children to live away from their parents and they would not have experienced much of court life, Greenwich proved to be just far enough away from London, but close enough should the royal children need to visit their parents on special occasions like feast days. Greenwich provided a safe and peaceful environment for the royal children to grow and a fourth daughter was born to the king and queen on 10 April 1472 at Windsor Castle, she was named Margaret and would have joined her brother and sisters in the royal nursery. There were many benefits to having the children away from court. For one, London was a hotbed for disease and illness and also the royal court was really no place for young children to be. It was often a busy and bustling place which meant the king and queen would not have had the time to spend with them, out in the countryside the air was fresh, there was plenty of open space and the focus could be all on them in terms of their upbringing. Their days would be fairly simple but they would have been structured as it would have been important that they had some order to their regime and play would have been equally balanced with learning and prayer.

Princess Elizabeth would have begun her formal education around the age of 5 or 6 years old and would have followed a similar pattern to that of most wealthy girls of her age. Although being girls meant they were not educated in academic subjects like young boys were, their path was different and more to do with the house and home. They were taught the skills needed to run a grand estate including how to run a household of many people. It was also important she be taught how to be a good and obedient wife, as that was her duty, regardless of if she was a princess, queen or a simple maid.

In order to run a successful household, she would have been taught how to read and write as any young lady would need to know all the ins and outs of their household expenditure, regardless of rank. They would need to be able to run their husband's estates efficiently, deal with any disputes that arose and write her own letters, it was her job to ensure the master of the house was not bothered with the trivial day to day running of things. She would also need to be a competent master herself for when her husband was away, especially if there was a war on and he was needed with his men on the battlefield although this may not have been something Elizabeth would have needed to worry too much about given the army of staff employed in the royal household that could assist her. She would also have received training in embroidery and sewing, Katherine of Aragon often mended her husband's shirts and embroidered gifts for him.

Like her father, Elizabeth was a great lover of reading, there is a devotional volume held in the British Library which Elizabeth has inscribed in her own hand 'This book is mine, the King's daughter' her father encouraged Elizabeth and her sisters to read, many men thought it a skill wasted on young girls but he and the queen were keen for all their children to be well versed and well educated in the skills they felt would benefit them most. Much of the practical learning Elizabeth and her sisters did came from simply observing her mother and other great ladies of the court. They would have taught them how to deal with people, how to engage with their staff and how to delegate duties fairly. Elizabeth was always considered to be kind and gentle with those who worked loyally for her, maybe we can assume her mother was the same.

The York sisters would be expected to make a good foreign marriage so knowledge of French, Spanish and possibly Latin would be invaluable, although there is no evidence to suggest that Elizabeth ever learnt Spanish and she struggled to speak French, although she could read and write in that language she could not hold a conversation in it and relied on interpreters. In contrast to the more practical subjects learnt by the princesses, their brothers would have been taught more academic subjects. The education of the princes would have been at the discretion of the king and he would have been much more involved in his son's learning than his daughters'. Careful plans would have been laid down in order to prepare Prince Edward for kingship and this would have started at a fairly early age.

A plan was laid down in 1473 when Prince Edward was just 3 years old. It was in this year that the young Prince of Wales was sent to Ludlow to establish his own court under the supervision of his uncle the Earl Rivers. At Ludlow he would learn to rule like a king and as Prince of Wales he needed to be near his own domains. It must have been difficult for the king and queen to pass over the care of their young son and heir to others so far away but both knew it was a necessary evil and one that could not be put off for too long. No doubt Elizabeth and her sisters missed him greatly when he left but he did return on a regular basis, especially for great feast days, Christmas and birthdays so he would have remained relatively close to all his siblings.

The trips home would also have been an opportunity for his parents to see how he was fairing in his new life; I am sure what they saw pleased them greatly. But it was not all about learning how to be a great lady in terms of running a household. Great ladies of the court also had to know how to dance, ride a horse and play a musical instrument as these were all considered to be accomplishments that helped to show how refined a lady was and how to attract an eligible bachelor. Her personal hygiene and eating habits were also to be scrutinised as was her sense of style for she had to dress well too. Her manners had to be beyond impeccable and naughty behaviour was not tolerated under any circumstances.

Thankfully both her parents placed great emphasis on educating not just their sons but their daughters too and this would be something Elizabeth would carry through when it came to her own children in their nursery at Eltham Palace. The good seeds sown in childhood often influence how the child then behaves in adulthood bringing with them what they learnt through to the upbringing of their own children. Elizabeth educated her daughters as well as her sons. King Edward had an extensive library and he allowed his children access to the beautiful manuscripts held within them. Elizabeth enjoyed reading and indulged in a wide range of topics, from religious texts to the Arthurian legends the king enjoyed so much and from them she would have learnt about chivalry and romance and would have dreamt one day about finding her own prince charming.

In September 1472 at the age of 6 years old Elizabeth was at Windsor Castle with her parents to welcome Louis de Gruuthuse to court. He was a nobleman and the Governor of Holland who had helped shelter Edward during his time in exile there. In honour of his loyalty Edward created him Earl of Winchester, It was important to Edward that he rewarded the loyalty of those who had served both him and the queen during her sanctuary. In 1471 he created Abbot Milling as chancellor to Prince Edward and Gould the butcher who had supplied fresh meat for the queen and her daughters was allowed to trade freely at any port for one whole year. Dr de Sirego was paid £40.00 (approximately £20,000 today) for his assistance during the queen's pregnancy and midwife Margaret Cobb was given a pension of £12.00 (£6,000) for her services during the birth of Prince Edward. During the visit of the newly created Earl of

Winchester, Elizabeth joined her parents at the high table for the celebratory state banquet, a perfect opportunity for her to show how well-mannered she was and to show off her dancing skills. It is said she danced with her father and the Duke of Buckingham to great applause.

It was clear to all at court that Elizabeth was turning out to be the perfect princess and in 1475 at the age of 9 years old she became betrothed to the Dauphin of France, Charles, who was aged just 5. Edward had invaded France with a view to conquering it but he later found out that his allies the Burgundians and the Duke of Brittany had reneged on their promise to provide support for his war efforts. This disappointment left Edward in an awkward position meaning he had no choice but to come to terms with France. King Louis XI of France and Edward IV of England met on 29 August 1475 on a bridge at Picquigny where they talked through a wooden trellis. The result of that discussion was the Treaty of Picquigny and from that came peace and the agreement of the marriage between Elizabeth and Charles. It also contained a payment of around 75,000 crowns which was to be paid immediately by France and that was to be followed up by an annual payment of 50,000 crowns.

When it came to the marriage negotiations the Duchy of Aquitaine, which had been in English hands for over 100 years, was to form part of Elizabeth's dowry and handed back to France. Once they had married and Elizabeth was settled in France, Louis would settle on her rents that totalled an annual sum of nearly £60,000, it was considered this would be the amount needed to keep her in the state of Queen of France. But this was a political marriage and contingency plans had to be made so it was agreed that if Elizabeth died before the marriage her sister Mary would take her place, evidence that young girls were often nothing short of a commodity in the political world.

It was agreed Elizabeth would leave England and travel to France when she was 12 years old, this was the age of consent for girls at this time, it was 14 years old for boys, so she had some time left at home in the care of her mother. From this point on Princess Elizabeth was styled as Madame Dauphine and this meant a new luxurious wardrobe and French lessons, the Queen of France would not be able to rely on a translator so a strict new regime was put in place ready for her to assume her new role when the time came.

The marriage of Princess Elizabeth to the Dauphin was a huge honour for England and brought pride and joy to her parents, what Elizabeth thought we do not know but at her tender age she probably felt daunted and scared at the prospect of leaving her home, her mother and her siblings. She would have to turn her back on England and take on the role of Queen of France but she knew it was her duty to honour her father's wishes and she would bear the burden well.

Whether her thoughts and feelings would have changed the outcome is unknown, her father was loving and cared deeply about his children but this was a matter of politics and war and the marriage had to stand. To further enhance Elizabeth's status, Edward made her a Lady of the Garter alongside her mother and aunt, Elizabeth Plantagenet, Duchess of Suffolk. The great ladies would have processed from Windsor Castle down to St George's Chapel. This is the most noble order within the English royal court so for Elizabeth to be included alongside her mother and aunt shows us how much love and respect the king had for his eldest daughter.

At this point in time, England was at peace, the King was popular and his court was lavish and exciting. England had good prospects and was becoming a European powerhouse but the queen and her family were still hated and the resentment ran deep. Warwick may be dead but there were still plenty of nobles that felt displaced by the Woodville clan and to them scores still needed to be settled. King Edward buried his head in the sand over the matter but there was joy as the royal children were growing in numbers. On 17 August 1473 a second son was born, Prince Richard, Duke of York was born in Shrewsbury and on 2 November 1475 another daughter was born to the king and queen, she was named Anne of York and was born at Westminster Palace. Princess Anne was followed by the birth of a further son, Prince George, Duke of Bedford in 1477. The royal nursery was complete by the birth of Princess Catherine in August 1479 and Princess Bridget in November 1480.

With the royal nursey full to bursting England and it's future looked settled and prosperous but there was always an under lying resentment bubbling between the king's family and his supporters and the ever-grasping Woodvilles.

Chapter Six

The Downfall of Uncle Clarence

Family was important to the king, he hated arguments and disagreements so the uneasiness between his own family and that of his wife unnerved him. In the July of 1476 the royal family moved to Fotheringhay Castle, the principal seat of the house of York to witness the re-burials of Edward's father and brother. Richard, Duke of York and Edmund, Earl of Rutland were killed at Wakefield in 1460, their bodies had been buried at Pontefract and York's head was sent to the Micklegate Bar, York where it was placed on a spike wearing a paper crown. But the time had now come to bury them both in the family plot at St Mary and All Saints, Fotheringhay. The bodies were brought to the church on the 29 July to be interred to lay at rest. After the ceremony Elizabeth went with her parents to distribute alms to the 5000 people that had gathered to pay their respects to the family.

Richard, Duke of York and his wife, Duchess Cecily had twelve children with seven of them reaching adulthood. The daughters had married well as was to be expected and the three surviving sons, Edward, George and Richard were left to battle amongst themselves for power. Richard, Duke of Gloucester (later King Richard III) married Anne Neville, the younger daughter of Warwick on 12 July 1472 at Westminster Abbey. Gloucester had been raised in the household of Warwick at Middleham Castle, Yorkshire and so would have known Anne from a young age making this more than likely a love match. Having said that, Anne would become one of the wealthiest heiresses in the land alongside her sister Isabel who was married to Clarence making the match a very lucrative one for Gloucester. Anne was a classic example of women being used as a pawn in the marriage market. She had firstly been married to Prince

Edward of Westminster when it was beneficial for her father and his cause but following Edward's death at Tewkesbury Gloucester requested permission from his brother the king to marry Anne, much to Clarence's anger.

Clarence decided to take drastic action to prevent this marriage by kidnapping Anne and hiding her away, he wanted to keep the Warwick lands to himself, he was not keen on having to share them out with his younger brother. Gloucester found Anne disguised as a maid in a house in London, the fallout between Gloucester and Clarence caused more family rifts, especially when Edward sided with Gloucester and awarded him a larger proportion of the Warwick lands. Clarence was livid with his brothers but in fairness to Edward, Gloucester had been loyal throughout the rebellion and joined him in Flanders, whereas Clarence was nothing but a trouble maker.

There was a spate of marriages in the house of Plantagenet when in October 1474 5-year-old Princess Cecily was betrothed to the future King James IV of Scotland who was aged just 2 at the time. The official betrothal ceremony took place in Edinburgh on 26 December, a proxy was used in place of Cecily. From that moment on she was styled as the Princess of Scots and her household was altered to accommodate the fact she was the future Queen of Scotland. The young Duke of York was married to the country's greatest heiress, Anne Mowbray, the sole heiress of the late Duke of Norfolk. She was 5 years old and the little prince aged just 4 at the time of their betrothal ceremony on 15 January 1478. Elizabeth and her sisters attended the ceremony along with Prince Edward who had come home for the celebrations at the Palace of Westminster with their parents. They all took their place under a golden canopy in the Queen's chapel. The queen led her young son to the alter and after the papal dispensations had been read out the king gave Anne away and the young couple were married. The marriage was followed by three days of festivities which saw the princesses giving out the awards for the jousting competition.

The marriage was a great occasion for the family, it was one of happiness and joy but that happiness was about to be shattered when

Clarence once again became the thorn in his brothers side. The only difference this time was the determination of the queen to finally bring Clarence to justice for his betrayal.

On 22 December 1476 Isabel, Duchess of Clarence died at the age of just 25, her death came just two months after giving birth to her son Richard and many believed she had succumbed to puerperal fever but others believed she had died of consumption. Her husband believed neither of these reasons and suspected foul play. It was his belief she had been poisoned by one of her ladies-in-waiting. The said lady was the unfortunate Ankarette Twynho and on 12 April 1477, four months after the death, around eighty men burst into her house where she was arrested and taken to Bath. From there she travelled on to Warwick where she stood trial accused of murder.

She came face to face with the duke of Clarence on 15 April at Warwick Guildhall where he put it to her that she had poisoned his wife by giving her 'a venomous drink of ale mixed with poison' and over the course of weeks watched as Isabel's health worsened, the jury found her guilty and sentenced to death. The speed of these events is frightening and shows us something of Clarence's state of mind around this time, he had the poor woman charged, tried and the sentence passed by midday, she was then taken from the Guildhall and executed immediately.

Author and historian Matthew Lewis suggests Clarence took this route as he saw his wife's death as a personal attack on him and that the world was out to get at him. Clarence comes across as someone who has been hard done to in his life, Edward took his throne, Richard took his lands and now he had lost his wife through 'poisoning'. Lewis also goes on to suggest that Clarence had wanted to remarry and that Edward had vetoed every candidate put forward. Clarence was looking for a new bride and one prospect was the stepdaughter of his sister Margaret of Burgundy. Mary was the only child of Charles the Bold who had died in battle in early 1477. It was a match that Margaret pushed for given that George was widowed and that he had always been the favourite of her brothers. Mary was a wealthy heiress and George would become leader of his own European fiefdom and the very prospect of him leading a European powerbase that was opposed to England was frightening. It put at risk the alliance England had reached with France and therefore prejudiced Elizabeth's marriage prospects. But more than that it would give him the opportunity to finally rival Edward for the throne of England, with the Burgundian army at his disposal and the North Sea open to his fleet the outcome could be disastrous for England and the royal house of York.

Edward rightly wanted his younger brother to have as little power as possible being given the slightest amount would spark another rebellion. His unpredictable nature could have put him on a collision course with England had he been allowed to marry into Scotland or Burgundy. Thankfully King Louis XI of France invaded the duchy of Burgundy and seized control of the area. On the one hand this stopped Clarence's power grab but it also gave Louis too much power. Edward was keen to remind the French king of their marriage treaty but he seemed uninterested, he had set his sights elsewhere. It became apparent Louis wanted his son to marry Mary of Burgundy, jilting Princess Elizabeth in the process. In the end Mary married Maximillian of Austria, the choice her father had suggested before he died and Elizabeth's future remained far from certain now Louis had shown his true hand.

In May 1477 a member of one of Clarence's households was arrested and sent to the Tower of London for questioning. Astronomer John Stacy was tortured into confessing that he had predicted the death of the king using black arts. During his ordeal he also implicated a man called Thomas Burdet, both men were tried, found guilty and executed for treason. This angered Clarence even further and fuelled the fire even more but Edward needed to send his younger brother a clear warning that this kind of behaviour would not be tolerated any longer. But Clarence clearly did not take the hint. The day after the executions had taken place, he arranged for a Lancastrian man named William Goddard to burst into the council chamber at Westminster where he had been ordered to regale the members with the scaffold speech of Burdet, once he had, the men left the room. When the news of this reached the king, he was furious with his brother and summoned him to Westminster to defend his actions. Edward gave his brother a stern talking to, but when he learnt that one of Clarence's men had used sorcery to predict the death of the king and the Prince of Wales, Edward's patience finally ran out. He accused him of treason and had him arrested and thrown into the Tower, where he remained for seven months, presumably to give Edward the opportunity to decide what course of action to take.

In January 1478 Parliament was called into session and asked to put Clarence on trial for a charge of high treason. Edward was to preside over the trial and Clarence decided to be his own defence. Did Clarence think he could win his brother round like he had done on so many previous occasions? Or did he think his time had finally come? Surely it must have crossed Clarence's mind as to why Edward was presiding himself, maybe the king had already decided his fate and the trial was just a means to an end. Edward opened by stating all his brother's previous brushes with traitorous behaviour, all of which he had forgiven him for and let's be frank and say had any other man committed the crimes would have lost his life much earlier.

But now there were new accusations for Clarence to defend, and they included Princess Elizabeth. Her uncle stood accused of plotting against the queen, Prince Edward as the rightful heir and all the royal children by requesting foreign assistance and the rebels at home to stir up trouble for the royal family, presumably with a view of removing them from power in favour of himself. Clarence had also encouraged members of his household to go about condemning the treatment of Thomas Burdet, saying he had been wrongly accused and executed unlawfully, he seems to have conveniently forgotten of his treatment of Ankarette Twynho, who incidentally was posthumously found not guilty of the crimes laid against her. Those who spoke publicly of Thomas Burdet and in favour of Clarence were paid well by the duke. Naturally the king was angry that his lawful judgement had been brought into question but this was just the start of the accusations.

Next, Clarence accused the king of being illegitimate, this story had surfaced before and had been used during the conflict with Warwick but the crux of this argument is, if Edward was indeed illegitimate then that made Clarence the lawful and true king of England. Edward was ruling with no lawful right to do so, I think this shows us the kind of person Clarence really was.

We know he was unstable, unpredictable and jealous, but to accuse your own mother of being unfaithful and knowingly allowing a usurper to sit on the throne shows just how desperate he was for power. The next accusation also calls into question the validity of Edward's reign. Clarence offered further examples as to why Edward should not be king and this one related to an agreement made during the reign of Henry VI. It states that should the king and his son Edward die childless then Clarence should be crowned, the shocking thing to consider here is that he would reign as a Lancastrian king rather than a Yorkist one, it would seem the House of York had splintered much further than first anticipated. For Edward, the most worrying thing here is that the laws made under Henry's brief return to power had not technically been repealed so in fact, Clarence could have been seen as the rightful king by law and Edward as the usurper. Clarence clearly had designs on Edward's throne and in order to shore up his bid he had supposedly made arrangements for his young son Edward, Earl of Warwick to be sent abroad, safe out of harms way should his power grab fail. The plan was to replace Warwick with another boy and the real one sent to Ireland or Flanders where he could be safely kept hidden away. It is an interesting idea but Margaret, Warwick's older sister at no time ever doubted the little boy she grew up with was not her brother.

The king may have considered forgiving Clarence had it not been for all the other earlier brushes with trouble but he had finally had enough, he was disappointed that his brother had yet again put him in the position and had thrown back Edward's goodwill. Clarence was convicted for high treason and sentenced to death. Many myths have sprung up surrounding the execution of Clarence, we do know that he was executed in private as befitted his rank but whether Edward offered him the opportunity to select his own method of execution we do not know and we certainly cannot be sure he chose to be drowned in a vat of Edward's favourite Malmsey wine. One thing we do know is that George, Duke of Clarence died on 18 February 1478 aged just 28 leaving his son and daughter orphans. The young Earl of Warwick was aged just 3 when his father died and due to the act of attainder he was barred from ever being able to inherit the throne or from claiming his father's land and estates, Margaret was aged just 5, both would suffer tragic ends. He was definitely the master of his own downfall, he was petulant, jealous and troubled but his death did not bring the end of the trouble for the king. Italian monk Dominic Mancini comments that the queen was behind Clarence's final downfall, out for revenge over the deaths of her father and brother, these accusations only heightened the hatred against the Woodvilles causing Edward more strife.

The rest of the family were shaken by at the execution and their mother, Duchess Cecily, spoke openly and protested that Clarence should have the dignity of dying in private which undoubtedly fuelled the rumours that have surrounded his death since. Although it was the reaction from his brother Gloucester that upset Edward the most. Richard felt Edward did not need to have had their brother killed, he could have kept him in prison in relative comfort, execution was such a final and decisive act. Following the execution Gloucester vowed to avenge his brother's death, he left court and went back to his northern strongholds, he blamed the queen and her family for his brother's death and that deep rooted hatred and resentment would come back and have a disastrous effect.

It is uncertain what Elizabeth thought and felt when her uncle was put to death but given she was under the influence of her mother she could hardly have had a favourable opinion of him. There are no records to tell us how much she knew of what was happening although she must have picked up on a certain level of tension at court. She turned 12 years old just days before the execution of her uncle and the time had finally come for her to move to France to be married to the Dauphin. Despite desperate pleas from her aunt, Margaret of Burgundy for Edward's help against the French, the English king was not willing to let anything stand between his daughter and her destiny of becoming Queen of France.

Chapter Seven

A Jilted Bride

The execution of the Duke of Clarence would not have been an easy decision for the king to make but left with little choice he did what he felt was needed to ensure the safety of the realm and for his throne. Edward could now turn his attention to the French alliance and the marriage of Princess Elizabeth and the Dauphin. Unfortunately, all did not seem to be well between Edward and Louis of France. The French king appeared to be stalling on the marriage alliance, despite Edward's pleas for him to move things along it seemed the French were no longer as eager for the match as the English. Edward was beginning to get frustrated and requested the jointure that had been settled on Elizabeth be paid to him without further delay. But we are talking huge amounts of money changing hands, the jointure alone amounted to £60,000 (in 2017, this was approximately £41 million using the National Archives converter) so it is no wonder Louis was stalling, especially if he had gone off the idea of an English marriage. He also stated the Dauphin was still too young at aged just 8 years old which considering the considered acceptable age for a boy to marry was 14 years old is a fair argument.

Frustration grew and the English advisors urged their king to pull out of the match but he refused point blank to even consider reneging on the deal. The match meant too much to just walk away from, both in terms of the money and the prestige and security a French alliance would bring, he would stick to his guns and continue to press Louis into going through with the deal. It soon transpired that Edward was right to be patient, his perseverance appeared to have paid off when Louis offered a part payment of £10,000. He did this because he was afraid of England turning towards Burgundy and forming an alliance against France, he had to act and so offered an amount that he felt would be enough to keep England interested whilst keeping France's options open. But for Edward, this was simply not enough, it was not what had been agreed as part of the treaty and he wanted what was due.

On the other hand, the Burgundians sat waiting in the wings to see which way England would go because they were looking at Elizabeth as a potential bride for their son Philip. It was clear to see that Louis was playing with Edward, he was making a fool of the English king by openly entering talks with Scotland over a marriage between the Dauphin and King James III's daughter Margaret. One can only imagine how this went down when this news reached the English court, Edward's response was to threaten Scotland with all-out war and thankfully this was a big enough threat to make the Scots back out of the negotiations leaving Louis with nowhere to turn.

By 1480, Elizabeth turned 14 years old and was described as virtuous, kind and beautiful, everything a princess ought to have been by the standards of the day. Her beauty was said to resemble that of her mother with flowing long blonde hair and a fair and clear complexion. She would have been a catch for any European prince but whether it was to be a French one remained to be seen. The wait to discover her fate went on but whilst she waited her education continued under the guidance of her mother, one thing for sure was Princess Elizabeth of York would be well prepared when her time to be a bride came.

Sadness engulfed the court in March 1479 when the 2-year-old George, Duke of Bedford died at Windsor Castle. He was the first of the king and queen's children to die in infancy and he was buried in St George's Chapel Windsor on 22 March 1479. The death of the young Duke of Bedford would have been an upsetting time for Elizabeth and her siblings, they had all grown up together in the royal nursery and George's death would have left a gap that would have been felt by his brothers and sisters. The queen was pregnant at the time of her son's death and on 14 August 1479 she gave birth to the couple's ninth child and sixth daughter, at Eltham Palace, she was named Katherine after her aunt. On 10 November 1480, the queen gave birth to her final child, a daughter named Bridget. The baby girl was also born at Eltham Palace and Elizabeth stood as godmother to her youngest sister who was destined for a life in service to God which was a decision that had been made either just before Bridget was born or shortly after her birth. It was not unusual for large noble families to offer one of their children to the service of God as a way of thanking the Lord for the number of healthy children He had granted them. Bridget never rebelled against this decision and was happy to become a nun at Dartford Priory where she remained in touch with her family.

The year 1480 also saw the betrothal of Princess Anne, a treaty was signed with Burgundy that she would marry prince Philip when she reached the age of 12 years old causing great concern to Louis as it now looked like England and Burgundy were uniting against him. In retaliation he stopped paying his instalments to Edward and prepared to go to war. Edward was busy negotiating marriages for his children and the most important was the betrothal of Edward, Prince of Wales. An agreement had been struck with the Duke of Brittany that his 4-year-old daughter Francis would marry the prince when she reached the age of 12, a future queen of England had been chosen. The 14-year-old Princess Mary was betrothed to the future King Frederik of Denmark and James III was now requesting Princess Cecily be sent north to Scotland to marry his son. Edward was making alliances right across Europe, extending England's power and influence far and wide.

For all his hard work, it would seem like that many of Edward's plan were not going to come to fruition. Sadly, Princess Mary was not to make her match as she tragically died at the age of just 15 years old at the Palace of Placentia in Greenwich. Her funeral was held at the Church of the Observant Friars before her coffin was taken to St George's Chapel, Windsor where she was laid to rest next to her younger brother George. Elizabeth was left devastated by her sister's death, they had been close in age and being the two eldest of the king and queen's children meant they grew up together, they were perhaps the only two old enough to remember the ordeal of sanctuary. Elizabeth had to face life now without her closest confidant. Things went from bad to worse when Cecily's betrothal to Scotland was called off after James III made a raid over the border causing Edward to retaliate and even Elizabeth's shaky union was in more doubt than ever before. Mary of Burgundy died in a riding accident and her people did not like her husband Maximillian so they turned to King Louis for assistance. On 23 December 1482 they signed the Treaty of Arras and part of that treaty included the marriage of the Dauphin and the 3-year-old Margaret of Burgundy and just like that, Princess Elizabeth of York was swept aside leaving her and England publicly humiliated. Although she may have been relieved that she did not have to leave her home the shame of being a jilted bride would have been difficult to shake off. When the news of the treaty reached the king in England he was said to be so enraged he called on Parliament to declare war on France.

Elizabeth had spent much of her childhood living with the prospect of becoming the French queen hanging over her. She had the worry of having to leave her home, her parents and siblings and everything she had ever known which must have caused her worry and anxiety. She knew it was her duty and because her father wished it she had no choice in the matter but when the agreement was broken she understood how humiliating this was for her and her country.

The embarrassment on such an international stage was more than she could bear but for all the shame she may have felt none of it was of her doing because just like arranging a marriage, the ending of a marriage agreement all came down to politics and had nothing to do with how the bride or groom felt. But soon enough a jilted marriage was going to be the least of the family's worries. The deep-rooted resentment that had plagued the royal family for years was about to implode, a storm was brewing that would engulf the House of York and bring it to its knees.

Chapter Eight

The Fall of the House of York

King Edward IV died unexpectedly on 9 April 1483 at Westminster at the age of just 40. No one expected the robust king to die when he did even though he had been suffering from a short illness. It was his untimely death that triggered a series of events that have gone down in English history as being some of the most controversial and talked about, even to this day. In his later years the king had lived a life of excess, he ate and drank too much meaning he was overweight and it has even been suggested he used emetics in order to allow himself to eat even more. This description of the king is very reminiscent of his grandson Henry VIII, he too ate excessively in later life and like Edward was described as being tall and handsome in his youth.

Edward fell ill at Easter and it is possible he may have caught pneumonia from a fishing trip he made, this weakened his already fragile body and he later had a stroke and passed away as a result. His body was taken by barge down the River Thames to Windsor where his funeral took place at St George's Chapel. He was laid to rest on 18 April in the chapel he had redeveloped and extended throughout his reign. The queen and princesses would not have been permitted to attend the service but Elizabeth would have mourned in private alongside her mother, sisters and grandmother Cecily as it was not considered appropriate for women of nobility to grieve in public.

The sadness of a monarch's death is always met with the joy and hope of a new king or queen taking the throne, they represent a new era for the country and the death of Edward was no different. Following the king's death came the accession of his eldest son as King Edward V, he was proclaimed king in London on 11 April and at that point all seemed to be as it ought to have been. There may have been some nerves given the new king's young age but Edward IV added a codicil to his will that clearly stated his loyal brother Richard, Duke of Gloucester was to act as Lord Protector until the young king reached his majority age which could be anything from 14 to 21 years old. On the face of it the accession of Edward V should have been smooth even with a Lord Protector but Gloucester and the Woodvilles did not get on. He resented the queen and her grasping family for their influence over the old king and he blamed her personally for the death of his brother Clarence and since then he had brooded on his northern estates letting the hatred build. But the Woodvilles were in a strong position and when the council agreed that Gloucester should not have total control but a more limited role that was aimed at supressing his power they were even more hopeful they could swoop in and crown Edward before Gloucester had even been made aware his brother was dead.

The feeling of hatred was mutual and in an underhand move the queen decided not to inform Gloucester, who was in the north at the time of his brother's death, that the king had passed away. She was clearly wanting to exclude him as much as she could to prevent him taking any control of the regency council who had set the date for the coronation of 4 May. This seems to be a hastily arranged date but was done in the expectation that Gloucester would not be able to travel south in time to have any influence. Luckily for Gloucester, Lord Hastings, who had served the House of York loyally and had been Edward's Lord Chamberlain, rode north and informed him of Edward's death and of the plans to deny his brother's wishes by the Woodvilles.

Hastings urged him to travel to London as soon as possible, he would need men behind him and a plan. Gloucester, grateful to Hastings for his loyalty, wasted no time and formulated a plot to try and intercept the king as he travelled from Ludlow in the west to London whilst in the custody of his uncle, Earl Rivers. It was certainly a risky plan but crucially the Woodvilles had possession of the king and they had made plans to get Edward to London in time for his coronation, he had a small army of men to keep him safe, but his Uncle Gloucester had other plans. The Woodville clan had been very clever following Edward IV's death. They tried to circumvent his wishes by excluding Gloucester but what they underestimated was the role Lord Hastings had to play, ever loyal to the House of York he was wary and opposed to Woodville rule. He watched them closely and kept Gloucester informed, he saw how members of that family had been appointed to high office and once young Edward was crowned he would be under their control and influence.

They made their move. Gloucester and Hastings joined forces with the Duke of Buckingham and the trio were ready to remove the Woodville faction once and for all. Buckingham was married to Elizabeth Woodville's sister Katherine but did seem to ally himself with Richard fairly early on. He has been painted as a slippery character and is considered to be one of the potential murderers of the Princes in the Tower, with a distant claim to the throne is it plausible he murdered the young king and his brother? More on that later for now they had to strike first and Gloucester was ready to make his move.

On 29 April he intercepted the young king's travelling party at Stony Stratford, Buckinghamshire. Initially all seemed friendly, it was just a happy coincidence they had all met there. That evening they shared a meal together, everything seemed friendly enough and there seemed no reason for the king's protectors to have any concerns. They were wrong, as by the following morning Gloucester made the decision to take Edward under his protection and to arrest those who had accompanied him thus far. He arrested Earl Rivers, Richard Grey, (Edward's half-brother), Sir Thomas Vaughan, (his chamberlain) and Sir Richard Haite and sent them north to his strongholds at Sheriff Hutton and Pontefract Castle. There was not much outside opposition to the arrests which could indicate to us that the Woodville's were not in favour and the people appeared to be supporting Gloucester's role as the Lord Protector. Unfortunately, the loyalty of the king lay with his mother and her family, he had never built a close relationship with his Uncle Gloucester as he had been based in the north and naturally preferred the security of his Uncle Rivers who had been with him since his move to Ludlow nearly ten years earlier. Italian Dominic Mancini was in England at the time and he reported that the young king protested at the treatment of his men but his protestations had little effect and the rest of his men were sent home. The young king now had to prepare to ride to London beside his Uncle Gloucester.

News of Gloucester's coup arrived in London on 30 April, the Woodville's were stunned. The queen had to think fast and as she attempted to rally support she found her family were lacking in that department, she had no option but to enter sanctuary once again with her daughters and the young Duke of York. The only difference was, this time she was alone, no one was going to come and rescue them and they found themselves at the mercy of Gloucester, her sworn enemy.

It must have been a frightening time for the former queen and her children, Elizabeth was of an age to fully understand the danger they were in, all they could wish for was that Gloucester would keep to his word and crown Edward. Thankfully the kindly John Eastrey, Abbot of Westminster took the queen and her children in to the safety of his own home at Cheneygates. The prospect of being in sanctuary and with the sudden loss of her husband caused the queen to have a breakdown and as the eldest daughter, Elizabeth would have been her mother's main confidante and carer to her younger siblings.

Elizabeth was just 17 when her beloved father passed away. With no marriage deal made his death left her exposed and vulnerable and at the risk of foreign interference. Edward left her 10,000 marks as part of her marriage dowry, although she must seek the agreement of her mother and her brother, the king, before making any betrothal. It was made clear to her that she risked the loss of the dowry should she act without their permission and guidance. Edward was well aware his eldest daughter was a valuable asset to the family, she was of marriageable age, beautiful and intelligent and would make an advantageous marriage for the benefit of the country, she had to be protected. Edward appointed Thomas, Lord Stanley as her protector, he was the husband of Margaret Beaufort and had known Elizabeth since she was just 5 years old. She clearly felt comfortable with this appointment, and often referred to him as Father Stanley and he, along with his wife, would play a significant role in Elizabeth's early adult life.

Elizabeth's bond with her uncle was much greater than the king's was and it would have been hard for Elizabeth to believe that it was her beloved Uncle Gloucester that posed the greatest threat to her mother and sisters. The hope had to be that once Edward was crowned then they would be released from sanctuary and welcomed back into the royal fold, they were after all the king's immediate family. Edward V arrived in London with his uncle the Lord Protector on 4 May and went straight to the Tower of London as was customary for a monarch prior to his coronation.

Edward seemed popular with the people and Gloucester was behaving as any noble would do toward their monarch, he was acting with respect and deference, he even made sure new coins were minted with Edward's image and that laws were passed in his name, on the face of it all seemed as it should be. The coronation had now been set for 24 June and the council were pushing for the protectorship to end on that date but Edward was still only 12 years old and would have needed someone to rule in his place until he reached his full majority.

Trouble was brewing, the ever-loyal and popular Lord Hastings decided to switch his allegiance to the queen, his reasons stemmed from his dislike of the Duke of Buckingham and his growing concern over Gloucester's true intentions towards Edward. To him, at the end of the day his loyalty lay with his king, regardless of his age and who his family was. During a council meeting at the Tower of London on 13 June Gloucester accused Hastings and others of deception. He accused them of conspiring against his life by aligning with the Woodvilles. With the councillors assembled Gloucester openly accused Hastings of treason and without a trial or opportunity to defend himself, Gloucester had his old friend Hastings dragged from the meeting and executed on the green outside. Mancini claims that

Gloucester believed Hastings and others had come to the meeting armed with weapons to attack and kill him. He did not stop there, he also had Lord Stanley, the Bishop of Ely and the Bishop of York arrested for treason, he sent them to Wales to be held as prisoners in various castles. Stanley proved too rich and powerful to keep locked up and he was soon released, he re-entered the council, as Elizabeth's protector it was paramount he had his freedom, she could not withstand to losing another of her father figures.

But what was the real reason for executing Hastings? He had been loyal to the House of York, just like his father before him. but was that in itself the issue? Hastings was loyal to Edward IV and therefore to his children. He supported Edward V as king, he clearly did not support Gloucester as king and he paid the ultimate price. The execution of Hastings may not be as clear cut as I have described above. There could well have been a plot against Gloucester's life and he was left with no choice but to accuse him of treason. Some historians suggest a trial was conducted at the Court of Chivalry where he was found guilty and executed sometime around 20 June. Gloucester knew he could not let Hastings live if he had desires to take the throne himself, he would prove too much of an obstacle to overcome to get to the throne. Hastings was buried in St George's Chapel, not far from Edward IV.

The tide was turning fast, Gloucester suggested to the council that Edward ought to be joined by his younger brother in the Tower and the coronation should not go ahead without his brother being present, he was after all Edward's heir. He suggested Prince Richard should be removed from the care of his mother in sanctuary and brought to the tower to join his brother but it was not going to be an easy task to convince the dowager queen to give up her son and send him into the hands of the man she thought was going to do them all harm. Gloucester argued that Richard would surely want to be with his brother whilst he prepared for his big day and sanctuary was no place for children, they should not be kept locked up against their will, which seems rather ironic given the events that are about to unfold.

The council tried to negotiate with the queen to leave sanctuary with her children, they promised her they would all be safe but she refused, not trusting the council, or Gloucester. On 16 June Gloucester had Westminster Abbey surrounded, he had come to collect Prince Richard, Duke of York and was willing to use force should his mother refuse to cooperate. He sent the Archbishop of Canterbury, Thomas Bourchier, in to sanctuary to try and negotiate with the queen, surprisingly she relented and released Richard into the care of the Duke of Gloucester on the premise he went to the Tower to be with his brother. The York sisters stayed with their mother in Cheneygates, much to Elizabeth's dismay, she longed for the freedom of the outside world, but their suffering was to last a while longer and there were more shocks to come.

Edward V and his brother Prince Richard were being lodged in the white tower where they were kept behind barred windows, the king's attendants had been denied access to him and they were slowly being drawn deeper into the Tower precincts. They became more and more isolated and seemingly becoming more like prisoners of the Duke of Gloucester. As June went on the two young boys began to be seen less and less and it was around this time talk of Gloucester becoming King began to circulate. What had prompted such a course of action from Gloucester? Had he had this plan in his head the moment he left the north of England? Or, did events beyond his control carry him to this point? On 8 June the Bishop of Bath and Wells, Robert Stillington contacted Gloucester with information that Edward IV had already been pre-contracted to another woman at the time of his marriage to Elizabeth Woodville, meaning that the king and queen's marriage was invalid and the children illegitimate.

The obvious question at this stage would be why had it taken him twenty years to air this news seeing as he had had ample opportunity to do so beforehand? He had even sworn allegiance to Edward when he was created the Prince of Wales, should that not have prompted him to speak up? The issue with Stillington was that he wanted to please whoever was in power at the time meaning he would not have wanted to displease Edward IV by calling out his marriage so he presumably decided to keep quiet. There were no witnesses to the marriage which ought to render the ceremony invalid and the lady in question, Eleanor Butler, daughter of the Earl of Shrewsbury, died in 1468 so was unable to confirm or deny the allegation. She too never raised any concerns when Edward married Elizabeth, nor when she married Thomas Butler. Naturally those opposed to Gloucester's plans said the pre-contract was nothing but a work of fiction and with no-one other than Stillington to back up the claims it should be dismissed and the coronation of Edward V should proceed.

Those in opposition to this story had a very valid point as the law at the time of this supposed marriage stated that there had to be at least two witnesses in order to make the union lawful in the eyes of the church, as this as not the case it is difficult to validate these claims. There is no solid evidence that this marriage ever took place and if Edward IV knew of it then surely he would have taken the necessary steps to have it dismissed as there is not a chance he would have threatened his children's future claims to the throne. Regardless of any of these details, Elizabeth Woodville married Edward in good faith which ought to have meant the children born of that marriage were legitimate.

Another interesting point is that when Eleanor Butler died in 1468, the two princes had not been born so we could say that the marriage between Edward and Elizabeth became valid when Eleanor passed away, making the boys absolutely legitimate. It is hard to imagine Edward would have allowed any stain of illegitimacy to lay on his children by Elizabeth. Bishop Stillington was clearly a Gloucester supporter and it is not beyond the realms of possibility that the two of them came together to concoct this story in a bid to discredit the king and queen and to ultimately destroy the young Prince of Wales' claim to the throne. It does seem rather convenient that this 'evidence' from Stillington makes its appearance at the time of Edward V's accession and many of his subjects thought it was highly suspicious too. To the people of London, Edward was their new king and they celebrated this in the streets upon his arrival in the capital, soon though questions were being asked about the young king's welfare. The lack of any tangible evidence really throws this story into question but before long Gloucester was declaring the children bastards at the cross of St Paul's, he also reminded people of the old story that Edward IV himself was illegitimate making the whole marriage saga a moot point. If he truly believed his brother was illegitimate then why bother with the Stillington farce in the first place? And why not have backed Clarence's bid for the throne when he could?

The illegitimacy of King Edward IV's children from his marriage to Elizabeth Woodville was officially declared on 25 June 1483 at the Guildhall. In attendance at the proclamation reading were lords, the Lord Mayor and as many people of London that could fit in the hall. The reason given was that prior to this marriage, Edward IV had been 'legally contracted to another wife'. On the same day Earl Rivers, Grey, Vaughan and Haute were executed at Pontefract Castle in Yorkshire on the orders of Gloucester. They stood accused of plotting to kill the Lord Protector (Gloucester), they were not afforded a trial.

The rendering of Edward's two sons illegitimate meant the next heir would have been Clarence's son, the Earl of Warwick but he had lost his claim following his father's attainder, leaving Gloucester the undisputed heir to the kingdom of England which he was urged to take by the councillors. The Lords and Commons however needed to be persuaded and Buckingham lent a hand leaving them with no option but to accept Gloucester as their new king. Richard, Duke of Gloucester, the fourth surviving and youngest son of Richard Duke of York and Cecily the Duchess of York, appeared to reluctantly accept the throne of England which he ascended as King Richard III.

A bill was passed in parliament titled the *Titulus Regis* which clearly states the basis on which Richard was claiming his throne, it is dated 26 June 1483. (see appendix three). He was crowned at Westminster Abbey on 6 July alongside his wife Anne Neville. As he prepared for his coronation at the Tower, could the young princes hear from their rooms what was happening below? How much had they been told about what was happening to them? Where they even still alive? Elizabeth must have felt huge sorrow for her brothers, she herself had lost her title and status, meaning a lucrative foreign marriage was unlikely to happen, and with no freedom it had all happened in such a small time frame of just under three months. It must have been a lot for her to take in but with her uncle Richard on the throne the future looked remarkably uncertain. There were rumours circulating of plans to rescue Elizabeth and her sisters and to take them into hiding, either abroad or in England but when Richard heard the rumours he put the Abbey under siege. His biggest concern being that one of the girls, probably Elizabeth, could gather enough support and attempt to reclaim the throne, and if she were to marry and have sons then Richard's grasp on the crown could become decidedly weaker. Elizabeth and her sisters posed a huge threat to Richard and his own family's safety, he was adamant no one left the Abbey without his prior say so.

It looked like Richard was sitting pretty on the throne, he had his queen by his side and his son and heir safely cosseted away in the north at Middleham Castle. But the cracks were beginning to show from an early stage, his grasp on the throne was fragile and only remained secure with the backing of the nobles. The unreliable Duke of Buckingham decided to switch his allegiance from the king, he was supposedly not comfortable with Richard's behaviour, given the king had made him Constable of England only a matter of weeks before this move does seem peculiar. Why the sudden change of heart from Buckingham? What did he know? Or, what had he done?

There have been many suggestions over the years regarding the disappearance and presumable murder of the Princes in the Tower, did Buckingham have them killed in order for him to make a claim for the throne himself? He would have seen that Richard was not overly popular, did he murder the young boys and accuse Richard of doing it to blacken his name even further? Or was he working for someone else? Buckingham did have a claim to the throne through his ancestor Edward III but it seems an odd time to make a claim for yourself, surely you would have done it at the time Richard made his claim, this scenario seems a longshot, especially given how much he had prospered under Richard's reign. However, the reliable *Crowland*

Chronicle states the October rebellion led by Buckingham and his kinswoman Margaret Beaufort, who had agreed to lend her support on the proviso her son Henry Tudor was permitted to return home from his exile in France, was the time when rumours were starting to spread that harm had come to the two boys. Some modern historians have tried to implicate Margaret Beaufort over the killing of Edward and Richard but there is no contemporary evidence at all to support this, it more than likely has been done retrospectively from the modern-day viewpoint knowing that her son did become king. That is not to say though that she was not part of the rumour mill which had the sole aim of accusing Richard III of murder and to discredit his name.

If we assume Buckingham had no hand in killing the two princes one likely answer for his abandonment of Richard is that he was uncomfortable with the treatment of the boys, maybe the king had confided in him regarding the issue of what should be done with the princes because whilst they lived they remained a focal point of rebellion, maybe this was a step too far for Buckingham.

So, what did happen to the princes in the Tower? That is one of English history's biggest questions that no one has the definitive answer to. Initially the princes had been seen playing in the grounds of the tower, then they were only seen at windows until finally the two boys retreated deeper and deeper into the Tower to the point they vanished from view. This was the account in the book *The History of King Richard III* that was written in 1513 by Sir Thomas More, but please let us bear in mind that Tudor propaganda surrounding Richard's life and reign was cranked up to the hilt as it justified the Tudor reign to make Richard as evil and villainous as they could. It was from books like these and plays by Shakespeare that give us our modern day perspective of Richard. It is certainly where we got the withered arm and the crooked back images from. Many believe Richard III had them killed to make his claim to the throne more secure, others believe they survived and were spirited away to safety by Richard, unable to bring himself to murder his own nephews. Recent discoveries made abroad lend weight to the theory that both boys managed to escape the Tower. Edward is said to have returned to England to claim his throne but was either injured or killed at the Battle of Stoke. Richard on the other hand is said to have returned under the guise of Perkin Warbeck, knowing his brother had died, he was the rightful claimant to the throne. Like the accusations that Richard murdered his nephews, there is no concrete evidence to support the theories the boys escaped but the new research certainly blows open the question of what happened to the Princes in the Tower.

Richard III had been loyal to his brother Edward IV so could he have been that hungry for power that he would have murdered his sons, his own nephews? He doesn't come across as the kind of man that would have wanted revenge so badly on the Woodvilles that he would kill their sources of power, he didn't seem a vindictive man and certainly not a man that would harm his own blood to win over on them. If he wanted the crown and to hurt the Woodvilles then making them illegitimate was enough to secure his throne, he wouldn't have needed to have them killed, but if they lived they would always have been a focal point of support for the Yorkist faction, even though Richard himself was of the House of York, one false move and Edward becomes a real prospect as an alternative Yorkist king, especially as he got older.

There is certainly support for both arguments and research is ongoing but Richard certainly seemed to have the most to gain from their deaths, he also had the means and the opportunity although if he did do it, it would not have been done by his own hands. One suggestion is that on the evening of 3 September the young boys were suffocated in their beds by a man called Sir James Tyrell who had been hired on the orders of the king. Tyrell had been in Richard's service for some time and was a loyal servant who was rewarded by being created the High Sheriff of Cornwall in 1484. He was certainly at the Tower of London around the time the princes are said to have been murdered because he had been sent there to collect the regalia for the investiture of Richard's son as Prince of Wales that was due to take place in York on 8 September. This all makes a compelling case and years later Tyrell is said to have confessed to the murders to Sir Thomas

More when he was writing his *History of King Richard III,* which like William Shakespeare's play *Richard III* undoubtedly had a healthy dose of Tudor propaganda thrown in for good measure.

There are many areas of this debate that concern me and whilst I have tried to be neutral and not get drawn to one side or the other as primarily I think there are sound arguments for it being and not being done at Richard's request. But if the boys were alive and well in the Tower, why not show them to the public? If someone else had killed them, Buckingham perhaps, then why not publicly accuse them of murder? At no point did Richard profess his innocence but also at no point did anyone accuse him of murder, even when Henry Tudor sat on the throne he did not accuse Richard. Maybe it was all down to the fact that no one knew where they were. If the boys had died of natural causes, again why would you not just state this to the public, why keep that news secret? The problem was there were two of them, if Edward died of natural causes, which he may well have done as there are reports of a doctor visiting him, it still left Prince Richard alive to take the throne, for anyone to take the crown from them, they both had to die. Maybe Edward V died naturally and only Prince Richard was murdered, maybe they both suffered from the same illness and they died just hours or days apart from one another.

Sadly, we will never know the full truth of what happened but when the bones of two young boys were discovered under a staircase in July 1674 during renovations at the Tower the mystery intensified. King Charles II ordered a casket to made to house the bones and they currently lie at rest in Westminster Abbey. There have been no DNA samples taken from the bones although tests in the 1930's indicated they were male and of the right ages for the princes. But these are not the only bones of children discovered at the Tower, two skeletons were discovered bricked up in an old chamber that have also at some point been claimed to have been Edward and Richard and when two coffins were discovered at St George's Chapel, Windsor in the vault of King Edward IV and Elizabeth Woodville many initially assumed it was of their son George Duke of Bedford and Mary Plantagenet, although their coffins were found, labelled in another part of the chapel. So, whose bodies lie in the unmarked coffins beside the king and queen?

There are many stories about Richard III that have been proved to be incorrect over the years, stories that were put about to sully his name. So, is the disappearance of the princes just another attempt to do this, just another false narrative put about by his enemies when in fact it was them that were the true perpetrators. His reputation was damaged irrevocably following the princes' disappearance and it has taken centuries for people to question the role he had, if any, over the mystery. One thing that is true is that Richard put aside the claims of his nephews and assumed the throne for himself, and that act alone fractured the House of York and its supporters.

The reign of Richard III is one of the most controversial in English history and he divides opinion to this day. Was becoming king part of Richard's plan all along, from the second he heard of his brothers untimely death did he plot to seize his nephews and steal their throne? Or was it a fight for survival, knowing the Woodvilles would strip him of his power and more than likely kill him, he had to do something to protect himself and his family that was certain. Richard was known for his loyalty to his brother, his nature was kind and chivalric, his motto 'Loyaulte me lie' (Loyalty binds me) speaks volumes. Could he really have killed his own flesh and blood to satisfy his thirst for power? If he had wanted to be king could he not have seized the opportunity when rumours about Edward IV's legitimacy were being bandied around, with Clarence dead it would have been an ideal opportunity to do so but he never made any attempt. Instead, he proved loyal to Clarence and to his memory by removing himself from court. Richard was known as King of the North, the northern people revered him as sovereign, he held vast lands and often protected the north and its people from Scottish raids over the borders. It seems he was happy with his lot in life and would have continued on in this vein had it not been for the early death of his brother.

But what of the Tudors? Did they have a role to play in the princes' fate? If Richard didn't kill them did someone connected to the Tudor faction do it? Margaret Beaufort was extremely keen for her son

Henry to take the throne and with Richard's reign looking shaky, did she seize on a moment to do away with the boys to clear the way for Henry to return triumphant? This seems highly unlikely as Buckingham had already written to Henry Tudor in France requesting his support in freeing the boys so why would his mother then go and kill them, the answer is, she wouldn't, she didn't need to. Or did they in fact escape with the help of loyal Yorkist supporters as recent research may suggest? But what is interesting to note is that Henry Tudor never publicly accused Richard of their murder when he himself became king. He also didn't hesitate in legitimising Elizabeth and her sisters in order to marry her as had been agreed but wouldn't he have only done this if he knew for certain the boys were dead? Tudor made a thorough search of the Tower when he became king in order to try and locate the boys but he drew a blank.

The death of the princes made Elizabeth the true heir to the crown, in the eyes of loyal Yorkist supporters but at just 18 years old and being female her chances of ascending the throne was defunct. It appeared that it was better to have Richard with his questionable claim than a woman. But if Elizabeth was to marry that could change everything. Buckingham had already made contact with Henry Tudor and it was Margaret Beaufort who planted the seed of uniting the houses of Lancaster and York through a marriage between her son and Elizabeth. This was a huge offer for Henry, Elizabeth was the heir to the House of York and would also bring huge support should he make a bid to claim the crown as the senior male of the line of Lancaster. Of course, all of this depended on the princes being dead but seeing as they had not been seen publicly for some time it seemed pretty certain they were no longer a threat and it was safe to make plans for an alternate ruler. But that nagging question always remained, without bodies how could anyone be certain they were dead? If the plan to unite the two houses was to work they would have to convince Elizabeth Woodville her sons were dead, she probably knew she would never see them again and had to look forward and the best way to do this was to see her daughter take the throne as queen.

The dowager queen and her daughters were still holed up in sanctuary at Westminster Abbey and Margaret Beaufort needed a way in if she was ever going to make this happen. In order to do this, she requested the help of her physician Dr Lewis Caerlon. He was to visit the ladies in sanctuary to break the news to them that the two boys had been murdered in the Tower of London by Richard but he could offer them no details of how or when exactly they died, he could not even give them the bodies to bury. This kind of news is earth shattering and reports state that when their mother had learnt of the princes' deaths she fainted, tore at her hair and pleaded with God to bring about her own demise. It was not just the fact that her two boys were gone but how could she reconcile the fact that she had given over her younger son to his murderer.

For Elizabeth to have to witness her mother's raw grief must have been extremely upsetting but she too would have to deal with her own loss, not only had her brothers died but it had been her once beloved uncle Richard that had sanctioned it. Princess Elizabeth would have to have been the sole comforter to her younger sisters given the grief of their mother, she would have to try and put aside her own tears and been strong for her mother and siblings. It was a lot for a young woman to shoulder but knowing what we do of her character she would have naturally wanted to comfort her loved ones and would put their needs before her own.

Through her grief Elizabeth came to see the benefit of agreeing to the marriage between her eldest daughter and Henry Tudor, if they wanted to exact revenge on Richard then taking this step was essential. On paper Henry Tudor was not a good match for Elizabeth, he had spent most of his life in exile in Brittany meaning he held no land in England or Wales and his title, Earl of Richmond had never officially been conferred on him. But what he did offer was an opportunity to remove the 'usurper' king and with Elizabeth's agreement plans were made to bring about the fall of Richard III.

Chapter Nine

The Rise of the House of Tudor

It had been agreed, Elizabeth of York was going to marry Henry Tudor. All Margaret Beaufort had to do now was inform her son of their plans and the potential prize his bride could bring him if he was willing to take a gamble. Buckingham wrote to Henry and told him to prepare to come to England to claim his bride and the crown, the date for the invasion was 18 October 1484 and Henry Tudor was all set to play his part. If the plot was to be successful they would need a lot more support than they had at that point. In England, Margaret Beaufort sent Reginald Bray to speak to those nobles they thought would join the plot. She also sent Hugh Conway to France with money and precise instructions for her son. The initial plan was for Henry to land on the southern Welsh coast and from there ride to join Buckingham at his castle at Brecon in the heart of Wales.

Bishop Morton, who had been held captive by Richard since the beginning of his reign, was released from his incarceration from Brecon Castle, presumably by Buckingham, and made his way to Ely in East Anglia, once there he was to raise as many men as he could to join the rebellion. Buckingham would recruit in Wales; the dowager queen's brothers Sir Edward and Richard Woodville would raise Surrey and their brother Lionel would raise Salisbury. The former queen's son Thomas Grey, Marquess of Dorset came out of hiding to raise men in Exeter. On the face of it, this looked like a well-planned attack, unfortunately none of the attacks were coordinated and before long Richard and his government learnt of what was going on giving them time to plan a counterattack.

On 15 October, Richard declared Buckingham a traitor and a rebel, his Welsh castle was surrounded and as soon as he left his home he was to be arrested. Unaware that he was surrounded, Buckingham left on 18 October as he attempted to make his way to Hereford but little did he know that his army had deserted him. He suspected something was not right so he made his way into Shropshire where he lodged with a retainer of his, sadly, this retainer's loyalty had a price and he betrayed his lord to the king's forces. He was promptly arrested and taken to Salisbury where the king was waiting for him. Unsurprisingly he was found guilty of treason and was executed in the market place on 2 November 1483. It was following his execution that Henry Tudor's name was first mentioned as a potential threat to Richard III's throne. Many of Buckingham's supporters pledged their allegiance to Henry and made their way to France where they began to plan a second invasion.

Henry Tudor had no idea of what was happening in England and sailed from Brittany on 31 October when news reached him of Buckingham's demise whilst he was docked in Plymouth harbour, he weighed anchor and set sail almost immediately. Henry's mother did not escape Richard's wrath, her property was taken from her and given over to her husband Thomas Stanley, a man who somehow managed to keep the peace with both sides. He was ordered to keep her under house arrest and away from the rest of the household so he sent her to his estates in the north of England at Lathom in Lancashire. To all the other rebels, Richard offered pardons but many had already fled across the channel to join Henry showing how seriously he was being taken as a potential candidate for kingship.

To reaffirm his dedication to the cause Henry went to Rennes Cathedral on Christmas Day with hundreds of his supporters to swear an oath that he would marry Elizabeth and unite the houses of Lancaster and York. The significance of this oath is hefty, it confirms his belief that Elizabeth is legitimate and the rightful heir to the throne and when news of the oath reached England it brought supporters from both houses together with a sense of determination that Henry was to be king, but only as long as Elizabeth was his queen.

Despite the failure of the October rebellion, the oath made by Henry must have brought hope to Elizabeth and her family in sanctuary. It gave Elizabeth's mother enough confidence to feel she could release her daughters into the care of Richard, she knew that if any harm came to them then Henry Tudor would avenge them. She probably also knew a second rebellion would come; why else would she take this action given the last time she trusted Richard with her children they ended up missing, presumed dead, but in reality just like the case with Prince Richard, did she have any choice? The dowager queen had to be realistic, Richard was young and if he managed to put down Henry Tudor for good then he could reign for many years to come. She also knew she could not keep her daughters in sanctuary any longer, it was not fair on them, they were girls of marriageable age and deserved their freedom. A source of security came in the *Titulus Regis* as it makes reference to the safety of the girls should they leave sanctuary, it was written into law that Richard would not harm his nieces and to be fair, he had no reason to harm them, they could be assets to him in the foreign marriage market.

Elizabeth and her sisters left Cheneygates on 1 March 1484, nine months after they had entered sanctuary, from there they went to join the court at Westminster Palace. The last time they had been there, their father was king and they were princesses, now their uncle sat on the throne and they were bastards, how they felt we do not know but one can only imagine it was a strange time for them and the loss of their father and brothers must have been tangible. Not only were they grieving for their brothers but they were concerned for the well-being of their mother who was still ensconced in sanctuary with no guarantees of her safety. They had no idea how long she would be forced to remain shut off from the world outside. But at the same time, they were free and dressed in their finery once more and that must have been a huge sense of relief. Finding a role for his nieces would have been tricky for Richard, as the bastard daughters of his brother, where exactly did they fit in at court? It is more than likely they went to join Queen Anne and her household, as unmarried ladies it was the only suitable role for them.

Queen Anne was the daughter of the old Earl of Warwick, her husband and brother-in-law's nemesis, she had been crowned alongside her husband but goodness knows how she felt when she rapidly went from Duchess to Queen in such a short space of time. Did Richard confide in his wife of his plans or was she left in the dark until the last minute? She was a devout lady and would often talk with her mother-in-law Cecily Neville about various religious writings, she attended Mass regularly and performed her role as queen as expected. She gave birth to her son Edward of Middleham in 1476 giving Richard his coveted heir but sadly he died in April 1484 after a short illness leaving the king and queen devastated. Anne is often described as meek and mild, uninfluential and has not gone down in the history books as being one of England's great queen consorts. Regardless of what did or did not happen during Richard's reign Anne stood by her husband, in what we can only assume was a loving marriage.

The former queen left sanctuary shortly after her daughters, there seemed little point in her staying now that all her children had left. Unsurprisingly, she did not join her daughters at court, even if she had been invited it is questionable as to whether or not she would have attended given her thoughts on the new king. Instead, following the removal of her property by the king, she was sent to live in the safe custody of John Nesfield at Heytesbury, Wiltshire and it was there that her daughters joined her. Nesfield was Squire of the Body to the King and was someone Richard could trust implicitly. It is said that Elizabeth wrote to her son the Marquess of Dorset in France and urged him to abandon Henry Tudor and any hope of Elizabeth marrying him, why she did this is unclear but maybe pressure from Nesfield played a part in it or maybe it was a decoy to throw Richard off the scent and to show her loyalty to the crown.

Henry Tudor was dealt a further blow the following January when Parliament ruled him a traitor. They stated that if he ever came back to England he would be arrested and executed, maybe the queen dowager felt anyone associated with the pretender would be tarred with the same brush and dealt with in the same manner. One thing was certain for Henry, if he came to England to invade then he had to be certain to win the crown, the alternative was almost certain death.

The Christmas of 1484 saw the York sisters return to the court of their uncle King Richard at Westminster, the contrast between the Christmases of just a few years before would not have been lost on them. Had it really only been just under two years since their father had sat in the great hall enjoying the court's festive celebrations? Yet now, he was gone, their brothers were presumed dead and their uncle sat on the throne and with them being declared bastards the future looked bleak. Despite this unfortunate turn of events Elizabeth was determined to make the most of the opportunities given to her. Elizabeth and Queen Anne got on well with the queen treating her niece as if she were a sister but Anne's health had suffered terribly since the death of her son, she was often melancholic and hardly left her rooms but as the Christmas season approached she was expected to perform certain duties beside her husband.

Rather shockingly it was about this time rumours started to circulate that Richard himself wanted to marry Elizabeth, despite his queen still being alive it was looking more and more likely that Anne was not long for this world. At one of the festive celebrations, Elizabeth and Queen Anne wore the same dress which was a huge insult to the queen. Sumptuary laws at the time governed peoples attire so that royalty wore only the most luxurious materials, only the king's family for example were allowed to wear purple and cloth of gold, the queen's gowns were expected to be the most sumptuous at court meaning Elizabeth, in her newly lowly status had no right to be dressing like a queen. It is also unlikely that Anne would have offered Elizabeth her gown to wear, Anne was a member of the Neville family, one of the noblest in England and she would have known the comments that would have been made had Elizabeth turned up at court wearing the same gown as the queen. If Queen Anne did not sanction the wearing of this dress then did Richard? If he did then it was done in very poor taste, knowing his wife was seriously ill and playing with Elizabeth's reputation in this way did him no favours.

Was he trying to discredit his niece in the eyes of the court, and more importantly Henry Tudor's? How much Elizabeth went along with the plan we do not know but from the king's perspective he looked cold and callous in allowing his queen to be humiliated in this manner.

The idea of Richard wanting to marry his niece caused a huge outcry at court. It would be considered an incestuous and ill-advised move on his part. The king should have been aware of this but according to sources he didn't seem fazed by the controversy he would cause. From his perspective she would have undoubtedly improved his standing amongst those who opposed his reign as she offered him some sort of validation as the true heir to the House of York. Marriage to Elizabeth could have helped the king's somewhat tarnished reputation and more importantly she could also provide him with his much-needed heir as it was very clear Queen Anne was dying and unlikely to lay with her husband again. But crucially, it would have ended any hope of Henry Tudor launching an invasion, but how seriously can we take this?

It is highly unlikely Richard wanted to marry Elizabeth, or any of his nieces, or vice versa. Was this just another move to blacken Richard's name, just another rumour to cause later generations to look upon Richard as evil and wicked? Let us think for a moment, he had made them illegitimate and so for a king to contemplate marriage to a bastard was unthinkable, he couldn't make her legitimate either without confessing his knowledge that the two princes in the tower were dead. It just seems so unlikely to me that Richard would have made any move against Elizabeth, even to save himself and his crown. She was his niece and he loved her, but only as a niece and would have done nothing to tarnish her reputation. But we cannot deny that these rumours did exist like so many that surround the reputation of King Richard III, I feel they should be taken cautiously. From Elizabeth's point of view this was certainly not a marriage she would have looked for. Not only was the uncle/niece relationship considered incestuous and would require a special dispensation from the Pope but she held Richard responsible for the death of her two younger brothers and

Elizabeth of York Royal Collection Trust © His Majesty King Charles III 2023.

King Edward IV Royal Collection Trust © His Majesty King Charles III 2023.

Elizabeth Woodville Royal Collection Trust © His Majesty King Charles III 2023.

King Henry VII Artist Unknown via WikiCommons.

Arthur, Prince of Wales Royal Collection Trust © His Majesty King Charles III 2023.

Margaret Tudor Royal Collection Trust © His Majesty King Charles III 2023.

Above left: King Henry VIII by Hans Holbein the Younger via WikiCommons.

Above right: Mary Tudor via WikiCommons.

Right: George, Duke of Clarence by Lucas Cornelisz de Kock 1495-1552 via WikiCommons.

Left: King Richard III via WikiCommons.

Below left: Margaret of York, Duchess of Burgundy. Sister to Edward IV via WikiCommons.

Below right: Cecily Neville, Duchess of York by Meister der Munchner Legenda Aurea via WikiCommons.

The Princes in the Tower by John Everett Millais 1878 via WikiCommons.

Perkin Warbeck. The only known image of the supposed Duke of York via WikiCommons.

The Pretender Lambert Simnel via WikiCommons.

Queen Mary I via Wiki Commons.

Young Lady Elizabeth via Wiki Commons.

King Edward VI via Wiki Commons.

Ruins of Sheriff Hutton courtesy of Carol Worster.

The Ruins of Middleham Castle Author's own image.

Above: The Tower of London via WikiCommons.

Right: Tudor Rose.

The Queen of Hearts playing card supposedly based on Elizabeth of York.

The Tomb of King Richard III, Leicester Cathedral. Authors own image.

for all the misfortune that had befallen her family since the death of her father. She seemed keen on marrying Henry Tudor, the stranger from overseas who will come and conquer and restore the country to greatness, a knight in shining armour if you will. But of course, as a woman Elizabeth would have had no say over who she married, if her uncle decreed she was to marry a certain gentleman from England or abroad, there was little she could have done about it, she would have to hope Henry Tudor got to her before anyone else did.

But it wasn't just Elizabeth's marriage that was on the cards, her sister Anne was betrothed to Lord Thomas Howard, the eldest grandson of the Duke of Norfolk. Unfortunately, it was not to be a happy marriage for Anne, he was unfaithful with his wife's own lady-in-waiting Elizabeth Holland and none of their four children survived childhood. Cecily did not fare much better; she was initially married to Ralph Scrope in 1485 with the support of her uncle Richard but this was soon dissolved by Henry Tudor as it was not a marriage that was seen to be in the interests of the new Tudor regime. She later married John Welles, 1st Viscount Welles and supporter and half-uncle of Henry Tudor. Sadly Welles, who was 20 years older than his wife, died in 1498. The couple did have two daughters together. Cecily would marry for a third time to Sir Thomas Kyme a Lincolnshire squire who was far beneath her in rank and status. The marriage was undertaken without royal consent which caused a rift between Cecily and the royal family. The couple moved to the Isle of Wight where their two children Richard and Margaret were born. Despite the controversy surrounding the marriage, they would remain together until her death in 1507.

Queen Anne finally succumbed to her last illness and died on 16 March 1485 at Westminster Palace aged just 28 years old, her cause of death is unknown but may have been as a result of consumption (Tuberculosis). The Queen was buried in Westminster Abbey and it is said Richard wept at her loss despite there being persistent rumours he had poisoned her in order to marry Elizabeth. The truth of the matter was that as King, he would need to marry again and once an appropriate period of mourning had passed, Richard sent Sir Edward Brampton to Portugal to negotiate two marriages. The first being for himself to the Infanta Joanna, daughter of King Alfonso V and the second for Elizabeth with Manuel, Duke of Beja, the king's own nephew and future King Manuel I of Portugal. Nothing came from either of these sets of negotiations but do these negotiations not tell us that Richard III had no intention of every marrying his niece?

Whilst the marriage rumours between Richard and Elizabeth spread, Henry Tudor spent his time getting ships, men and armoury ready to bring to England as part of his invasion. King Charles VIII of France offered Tudor his support and having that kind of backing made him a much bigger threat to Richard than he had first anticipated. But Henry had heard the rumours circulating at the English court causing him great worry. If Elizabeth did marry Richard then he would more than likely lose much of his support and be left as an exile in France. Despite reassurances from his mother that the plan was still going ahead he must have had concerns over what kind of reception he would face in England.

The rumours needed to be either confirmed or denied and on 3 April 1485 according to the *Crowland Chronicle*, Richard III made a public declaration that he had no plans of marrying his niece. He did this in front of the people and Mayor of London at the great hall of the Priory of the Knights Hospitallers of St John in Clerkenwell, he even went as far as claiming he had never even thought of the idea. If he hadn't then it begs the question as to where the rumours started in the first place, it seems an odd rumour to spread as it didn't seem to benefit either side. If you were on the side of the king then a rumour like that just blackened his name, if you sided with Tudor then it just caused unrest and uncertainty. It does paint Richard in a bad light but we are viewing it in hindsight but at the time it must have seemed an odd rumour to start. The news of the king's denial was sent across the country but it did not signal an end of the rumours surrounding him. Many courtiers truly believed he had poisoned his wife the queen and caused her great mental anguish in her last weeks. Allegedly the royal couple argued on a daily basis, Richard supposedly bemoaned the fact she was unable to get pregnant, yet he shunned her bed, it appeared that the queen was slowly dying in open view of the court and if we are to believe the reports from the time her husband did very little to ease her suffering. But we must bear in mind that these were just rumours, nothing was ever proved against Richard in terms of the treatment of his wife, just like it has never been wholly proved he killed the princes in the Tower.

But, as in most cases, the winners write the history books and Richard's reputation was damaged almost beyond repair by the incoming Tudors. Henry's supporters went about tarnishing the king's reputation and before long more men came over to Tudor. But what were the accusations against Richard? Well firstly and most importantly he stood accused of usurping the throne of his nephew and killing him and the Duke of York in the process. He also supposedly murdered his wife and condemned his brother's children to a life of illegitimacy but then tried to marry his niece. He also committed various acts of tyranny and lied to his nobles to gain and keep power when in reality his main powerbase was in the north and that was in part down to the fact he had married a Neville. Now that Anne was dead he potentially ran the risk of losing that support, especially if the reports of him murdering her were circulating.

There are many theories as to Richard's character, traditionalist Ricardians have him as a kind and loyal brother, which we can prove as he went into exile with Edward when he lost his throne temporarily and took care of the north of England for his brother. Edward obviously trusted Richard as he named him sole protector of his son and heir and the fallout from that could be interpreted as Richard being someone who acted to protect himself and his family. Richard has been very much maligned by the later Tudor propaganda, most notably by William Shakespeare whose play, *Richard III,* portrayed him as a hunch-backed tyrant with a withered arm and that image has stuck. Or at least it did until 2012 when a team from the archaeological department at the University of Leicester and the Richard III Society discovered remains in a carpark in Grey Friars Street in the city. Following DNA and forensic tests the skeleton was proved to be that of King Richard. Crucially it showed he did suffer from scoliosis of the spine which may have caused one shoulder to be higher than the other. However, there was no withered arm and experts advised that when the king was fully clothed it would have been difficult to tell he had any spinal issues at all. The extreme curvature of the spine and the withered arm were all tools used by Shakespeare to mark out Richard's supposed evil character but thanks to the efforts of Philippa Langley, the search manager, we now know the true facts of Richard's physical form. Back in medieval England any kind of deformity was seen as a stain on your character, a punishment from God if you will, and since then Richard's character has had to fight the accusations laid at his feet for nearly 500 years. I am not here to claim one way or the other that the crimes he was accused of were true, I will leave that to historians with a much better understanding of Richard and his life but what I will comment on is that the arguments put forward by Ricardians to clear his name are plausible and should be given credence especially given the fact that new evidence may have been found to clear his name of the murder of the princes.

In the spring of 1485 Elizabeth was at a loose end. Henry was still in France, the Portuguese marriage negotiations were off, she was 20 years old with no clear idea as to what the future had in store for her. She may have felt angry at not having her marriage sorted and she had no father figure to guide her until she turned to Lord Stanley. Thomas Stanley was Henry Tudor's step-father and had been named by Edward IV in his will as the person Elizabeth should turn to for guidance. He may have felt some resentment towards Richard following the treatment of his wife, Margaret Beaufort, but he offered a steady hand and remained on relatively good terms with the king. But what were Elizabeth's true thoughts and feelings at this time, was she desperate for Henry to attack or was she secretly wanting a marriage with her uncle? *The Song of Lady Bessy* is a ballad that was more than likely written by a member of Stanley's retinue. It charts Elizabeth's involvement in the run up to the Battle of Bosworth in August 1485 although it has been described as yet more Tudor propaganda in an attempt to tarnish Richard's reputation, but none the nonetheless it gives us a possible insight into how she felt during that fateful summer.

It begins with a scared Bessy complaining to Stanley, the man her father had entrusted with her care, that Richard had murdered her younger brothers in the Tower and his wife Anne in order that he may become king and marry her. Bessy sees this as an incestuous act and claims she wants revenge on Richard and declares her support for Henry. She calls on Stanley and his family to help her overthrow Richard, he answered Bessy's call and brought down his soldiers from his home in Lancashire and across the north of England, she also claims Gilbert Talbot a younger son of the 2nd Earl of Shrewsbury and John Savage, a close friend of the Stanley family, would offer their support too. As ever Stanley was cautious, he was a man who never truly gave his public support to anyone until the very last moment to ensure he was on the winning side. He urges Bessy to take into consideration that if Richard learnt of the plot, like he did before, she could be charged with high treason and if he murdered his nephews, he would not hesitate to do the same to his niece. But Bessy is determined to exact her revenge and reminds Stanley that she is the rightful Queen and the Head of the House of York, he offers to come to her secretly to discuss this matter further.

Stanley arrives as promised and tells Bessy to write to his brother, Lord William Stanley, in which she will plead with him to raise as many men as he can and to write to his own three sons to request the same. They were to meet along with Talbot and Savage by 3 May. The letters were given to Humphrey Brereton along with a small purse of coins. He successfully delivered the letters, firstly to Lord William at Holt Castle on the English-Welsh border, then to Lord Strange at Lathom in Lancashire and finally to Edward and James Stanley in Manchester. They all rally to the request although Savage agreed reluctantly having been a loyal ally to Richard in the past. Brereton returns to tell Elizabeth and Stanley that he has been successful in his request. The meeting was to take place at an inn on the outskirts of London. They all arrived and agreed to help Elizabeth by pledging money and men to bring Henry Tudor to invade and conquer England. The next stage of the plan was to send Brereton to France with a ring that he was to pass to Henry from Elizabeth. He was to meet Henry just outside the town of Rouen, it is said when Brereton handed Henry the ring he kissed it three times, this was Elizabeth's signal that she intended to marry Henry. Henry's reply was that he could not give an answer for three weeks as he needs to travel to Paris to secure the support of the French king, he later returns to confirm he will marry Elizabeth and make her Queen of England.

How much of this is true is uncertain but the *Song of Lady Bessy* offers us a small insight into how the events of 1485 might have taken place. Whether Richard ever suspected Elizabeth of plotting against him we do not know for sure but he could not have missed the fact that loyal Yorkist supporters claimed she was the rightful monarch of England and that she was a figurehead for them. Worried she may be a rallying point for war he sent Elizabeth away from court and decided to move her to his northern stronghold of Sheriff Hutton where he felt he could hide her away in the hope she would not be found. He claimed to do this for her own safety but he knew the bulk of his power lay in the north and would be more inclined to support him when the time for war came.

It must have been a frightening time for Elizabeth as was once again she was separated from her mother and sisters but there was some light relief at Sheriff Hutton as she joined her cousins Edward, Earl of Warwick and his sister Margaret, children of the Duke of Clarence, and the bastard son of Richard, John of Gloucester. Sherriff Hutton was under the control of John de la Pole, Earl of Lincoln, he was Richard's Lieutenant in the north and the eldest son of Richard's sister Elizabeth and her husband John de la Pole, Duke of Suffolk. Following the attainder against the Duke of Clarence, the young Earl of Warwick lost his claim to the throne so John de la Pole became King Richard's closest living male relative and was often talked of as being his heir although he was never publicly proclaimed Prince of Wales. He did however have the income from the Duchy of Cornwall conferred on him and this is traditionally given to the heir to the throne.

The time for war had come. On 1 August 1485 Henry Tudor left France with his invasion fleet. He set sail from Harfleur on the Normandy coast and arrived six days later at Milford Haven on the Welsh Pembrokeshire coast. As his soldiers disembarked on to the beach he urged them to march onwards which they did under a green and white banner which was emblazoned with the red dragon of Cadwaladr the legendary King of Gwynedd, from whom he claimed descent. As Henry marched his troops out of Wales and into England, Richard based his camp at Nottingham. Although by the time news of Henry's arrival had spread the king was losing much of his support. Not many answered his rallying call and the Mayor of York sent a paltry eighty men to join the fight, if the north could not answer his rallying cry to arms then King Richard was in big trouble as he was relying on that loyalty to bolster his numbers. One problem he faced was Henry could boast the whole of Lancastrian support and those disaffected Yorkists whereas Richard had only the remaining loyal men of York to call on.

Henry officially entered England at Shropshire on 15 August, this prompted Richard to gather his men and ride to meet him, the two armies clashed at Bosworth field just outside the town of Market Bosworth, Leicestershire on 22 August 1485. The Battle of Bosworth lasted just two hours, it has been estimated that a total of 20,000 men clashed that day and despite his loss of support Richard still commanded the majority of the men. Richard joined his men on the battlefield although Henry sat on the sidelines leaving the fighting to John de Vere, Earl of Oxford. The odds many have been stacked in Richard's favour in terms of numbers but Lord Stanley had yet to join the battlefield. He took up a position to the north side of the field and bided his time. He wanted to see which way the fight was going to go before committing himself even if that meant going against his stepson.

As the day of the battle dawned the king requested Stanley visit him in his tent, Richard had previously taken custody of Stanley's son and heir George, Lord Strange, as security for allowing Stanley to return to his home in Lancashire. Now Richard was using George as a bartering tool, if Stanley wanted to see him alive again then he would accept the summons and go to his king immediately. Rather brazenly Stanley advised the king he would not be attending him and that he had other sons! It was a huge gamble, Richard had already shown that he was not frightened to kill those who threatened him, he ordered for Lord Strange to be executed but the king's captain refused to carry out the order, instead he was to be kept under a close guard. Richard would decide his fate once the battle was done and Stanley had shown his allegiance.

The battle started well for Richard but it did not last long. When he saw his men were struggling in the marshy fields he requested the assistance of the Earl of Northumberland and his men, one of his loyal northern lords Richard would have been sure of his help but to his dismay Northumberland and his men stayed put and refused the order. Deserted by Northumberland the king felt there was nothing left to do but to make a charge of his own. He gathered around him a small band of loyal men and headed straight for Henry Tudor. He got as far as cutting down his standard bearer Sir William Brandon but before he could get any further Stanley entered the fray and sided with his stepson. Stanley's appearance was enough to seal victory for Tudor and to condemn Richard. The king was cut down 'like a brave and most valiant Prince'. There are many myths that have sprung up from Bosworth as to what happened after the king had been slain. His crown supposedly fell from his head and rolled under a hawthorn bush, Stanley picked it up and placed it on the head of Henry Tudor with all the soldiers around shouting 'God Save King Henry!'.

Richard III's mutilated body was taken from the battlefield on the back of a horse where it had been cruelly and callously flung. It was taken back to Leicester where it was put on display for two days giving people an opportunity to see the king was dead. He was later buried at Greyfriars church but his tomb was destroyed during the reformation and Richard's burial site remained unknown for over 500 years. That was until his burial site was found under a car park in 2012, he was later laid to rest in Leicester Cathedral in a religious ceremony lead by the Archbishop of Canterbury Justin Welby. Also in attendance representing the Royal Family was Prince Richard, the Duke of Gloucester and his wife Birgitte, the Duchess of Gloucester alongside Sophie, the Countess of Wessex (now Duchess of Edinburgh).

Henry Tudor was triumphant and the Tudor age had now begun with the reign of King Henry VII. But a king needs a queen and the time had come for Elizabeth of York to take her rightful place on the throne of England albeit next to a Lancastrian king. The wars of the roses was over and the houses of Lancaster and York were to be united at last in peace.

Chapter Ten

A Bride at Last

Henry Tudor was born on 28 January 1457 at Pembroke Castle, Wales. He was the son of Edmund Tudor, 1st Earl of Richmond and Lady Margaret Beaufort. Sadly, Edmund died three months before his son's birth making Henry the Earl of Richmond from birth. With his father dead and his mother just 13 years old, Henry came under the protection of his uncle Jasper and was later transferred into the care of William Herbert, the Earl of Pembroke. When Henry VI was restored to his throne Jasper took Henry to court but it was not to last as when Edward IV returned to reclaim his crown Jasper fled with Henry to Brittany, France leaving Margaret at home.

Described as being slender and lean yet tall and strong, by all accounts Henry VII was an attractive man with blue eyes, blond hair and a fair complexion. He had a cheerful disposition and was often seen smiling and laughing but there was a darker side lurking beneath the calm exterior. He was suspicious of those around him, he banned the private ownership of large armies and reinstated the Court of Star Chamber which ensured those lords breaking the law were suitably punished.

Henry could be devious as well as calculating but at the same time he was an intelligent man with a good sense of economics. Many accused him of being miserly and cruel in his later life but in his early reign he was witty and hardworking. Many respected Henry VII but few loved him but he brought a sense of stability to the country by establishing a strong government and a healthy economy. He made England a powerful nation in Europe and established good foreign trade links. Despite his hard work his reign would be eclipsed by those of his children and grandchildren who all built on the legacy he left.

Before Henry VII left Leicester on his triumphant return to London, he sent Sir Robert Willoughby and Sir John Halliwell north to Sheriff Hutton to bring Elizabeth south to London. They were also to take custody of the 10-year-old Edward, Earl of Warwick and his sister Margaret but they were to travel under secrecy as Warwick was seen as a threat to Henry's reign. The life of the Earl of Warwick is a tragic story, after arriving in London he was briefly lodged at the home of Margaret Beaufort, Coldharbour. From there he was then escorted to the Tower of London where he was cut off from his family and friends, he would spend the rest of his life locked away all because he may have been considered a figurehead for a Yorkist rebellion. In contrast to the Clarence children, Elizabeth arrived in London to a huge fanfare, she had an escort of noblemen and was taken to the home of her mother where she was reunited with her and her sisters. It must have been a joyous occasion for them all after so much uncertainty and worry living under the rule of Richard III they could now relax and be free. All Elizabeth had to do was sit and wait for Henry to summon her.

The new king entered London on 3 September 1485 and went straight to St Paul's Cathedral where he was to give thanks for his triumphant victory and for the throne that victory brought him. From there he rode to the Bishop's Palace where he held his first ever Privy Council meeting. He remade his declaration to marry Elizabeth but before he could there was some housekeeping to be done. Firstly, he needed Parliament to reverse the *Titulus Regis* to make Elizabeth legitimate again, this was an absolute must if he was to hold his side of the agreement and marry her. The second thing was to issue a dispensation that included Elizabeth's agreement to the marriage. It was all fine and well to reverse the *Titulus Regis* to make Elizabeth a legitimate bride but he could not reinstate her legitimacy without doing the same for her siblings and that meant the Princes in the Tower. To me, it is clear that Henry found nothing when he made his search for them, if he had found bodies then you would have expected him to have shouted it from the rooftops in order to blacken Richard's name further. Alternatively, finding nothing would mean there was a chance they could be alive leaving his reign open to question. Instead, Henry VII makes no reference to the young princes at all, he never publicly accused Richard III of their murder so he either had no idea where they were or what had happened to them, or, he knew exactly what had happened and wanted to leave the subject well alone and let the people believe Richard had ordered their murder. There was no point in reminding people of them, it would only serve to reignite the mystery surrounding their disappearance and supposed deaths.

Henry Tudor's claim to the throne was very weak, so it had been agreed that he was to claim the crown of England on the understanding he was to marry Elizabeth, the heiress to the House of York. She would add the legitimacy to his somewhat tenuous claim so when the news came that he claimed the crown in his own name at Bosworth Elizabeth was concerned. From her mother's home she went to lodge with Margaret Beaufort at Coldharbour where special rooms had been put aside and prepared for her. Sadly, it looked like she was in for a long wait, Henry seemed in no rush to marry her, for him it was important to establish his reign in his own name and right before she was brought into the mix, he needed the people to see him as a king who owed his crown to no one but himself. In order to cement this, he arranged for his coronation to take place before his marriage to Elizabeth, he had claimed his crown by conquest and did not need the Yorkist princess to legitimise his claim which he took from his mother as the Lancastrian male heir. Henry VII was also keen to focus on his ancestry from the great King Arthur and the Welsh Prince Cadwaladr, King of Gwynedd.

Being seen as king in his own right meant so much to Henry that he even dated his reign to the day before the battle of Bosworth which made all those fighting on the side of Richard III traitors. Naturally many of the men changed sides pretty much straight away, including the one-time heir to the throne, John de la Pole, Earl of Lincoln. Surprisingly Henry gave him a place on the council and he pardoned many of the others. Henry was a king who was paranoid and clearly wanted to keep an eye on any potential rival but the reluctance to marry Elizabeth straight away was a matter of concern for those Yorkist supporters who based their loyalty on the fact that he was to marry her. The marriage between Henry and Elizabeth was seen as the defining moment that brought the houses of Lancaster and York together and in doing so would bring to an end, years of war. His ongoing reluctance to marry her came across as a slight on her character, it looked like he had duped the Yorkists into supporting him and had betrayed Elizabeth in the process. Pressure built on Henry and he relented, he moved to Baynard's Castle which was just a short distance from Coldharbour and Elizabeth. This put them in close proximity and gave them the opportunity to spend time together and get to know one another in a more private setting. Soon love blossomed.

Henry VII was crowned King of England on 30 October 1485 at Westminster Abbey. Elizabeth did not attend the coronation so his mother took on the role of first lady in her place and would take the title of My Lady the King's Mother, it would be a further two years before Elizabeth was crowned. It was only after he was safely ensconced on his throne that Henry repealed the *Titulus Regis*. He ordered that every copy be destroyed except the original one which is how we know what it detailed. The aim of the destruction was to rid every last trace of the accusation of illegitimacy against Elizabeth and her siblings for if any stain remained on the queen then that would call into question her claim to the throne and in turn any children she may have with Henry. Once the *Titulus Regis* had been repealed Elizabeth automatically became the heir to her father King Edward IV meaning she technically should be the queen regnant of England.

Whilst salic law did not exist in England Elizabeth had every right to claim the crown in her own right but as a woman many believed she did not have the requisite skills to rule a country on her own. Unsurprisingly, men found it unnatural for a woman to have power over them and so female rule was discouraged, especially if an acceptable male alternative was available. In this instance, Henry was that preferred option and so even though Elizabeth was technically the country's first Queen regnant it was felt she would need a man beside her to help guide and make decisions. As the crown belonged to Elizabeth it should have been something she brought to the marriage enabling her husband to rule jointly with her but by having himself crowned before the marriage it became something Henry gave to her. Elizabeth never seemed to argue this point, there was never any support for her taking the crown for herself and whilst it irked some no one seems to have pressed Elizabeth to claim her birthright.

Many benefited after Henry's coronation, Elizabeth Woodville was finally vindicated and recognised as Edward IV's true wife and queen, she had her property and lands reinstated to her and finally received her widows jointure of thirty manors plus rents. His stepfather, Lord Stanley, was created Earl of Derby, Constable of England and Chief Steward of the Duchy of Lancaster. Henry's uncle Jasper Tudor who was instrumental in getting his nephew to the throne was created Duke of Bedford and married Elizabeth's aunt, Catherine Woodville.

On 10 December 1485 Henry officially announced in parliament of his intention to marry Elizabeth. The council and nobility were getting restless at his continuing delaying tactics over the marriage but now the *Titulus Regis* had been repealed there was no excuse for the marriage to not take place. They wanted her as queen and Henry could delay no longer. On the face of it looked like a love match, the couple had been spending time together and it was clear Elizabeth was in love. Henry was taciturn and saw the marriage as a political match that would bring peace and harmony to his realm. The date was set for 18 January 1486 at Westminster Abbey, from the moment Parliament agreed to the match Elizabeth was treated as queen and at the command of the king preparations were to be made for the wedding ceremony.

Elizabeth of York was 20 years old when she married the King of England at Westminster Abbey. The ceremony was led by the Archbishop of Canterbury, Cardinal Thomas Bourchier. The bride wore a gown of silk damask and crimson satin. Her kirtle was made from white cloth of gold and her mantle was trimmed with royal ermine. The groom wore cloth of gold and rings of solid gold were exchanged. This was a wedding ceremony the whole country celebrated, it had brought huge celebrations to London with bonfires being lit and singing and dancing in the streets. A large banquet was held at Westminster Palace followed by more feasting and jousting, the wedding night took place in the painted chamber within the palace. The red rose of Lancaster and the white rose of York were finally united, from this came the now iconic image of the Tudor Rose.

Elizabeth woke on the morning after her wedding day as Queen of England, she had finally reached her destiny. From birth her fate was to become a queen it had been a role she had trained for her whole life and now her time had come. Once the 'uprising' of the bride had taken place the new wife would have had her attendants dress her, one difference to being a maid was that her hair had to now be bound up and hidden under a hood as her long golden locks now became something only her husband could admire. Once dressed her duties as wife and queen could begin.

Chapter Eleven

Elizabeth, the Wife

As a wife and queen Elizabeth now found herself with a large household to run and many charitable causes looking for patronage. As a queen she would have the privilege of being able to support as many good causes as she could and be able to support and advance her family to higher positions in court. It was a lot to take in, despite being trained for this role since birth, her life changed overnight. Thankfully she had her mother close by to guide her when she needed it and Henry's mother, the formidable Margaret Beaufort, Countess of Derby, a woman Elizabeth would have to get along with if she was to have any influence over her husband. Despite having been separated from her son for many years during his exile, Margaret Beaufort remained Henry's biggest supporter and champion and throughout his reign she was the first person he turned to for advice. Elizabeth would have to forge a good relationship with her mother-in-law if she was to get close to Henry and in the early days of her married life all appeared well.

Elizabeth and Henry were both known for their generous nature when it came to looking after the less fortunate. They both gave alms to the sick and poor and both were devout in their religion. As queen, Elizabeth chose 'Humble and Reverent' as her personal motto, she also adopted the symbol of the white rose as her personal emblem, the symbol of the House of York. It must have been a challenging time for Elizabeth, she had to adjust to becoming queen and everything that role brings but she was also a new wife and that in itself brought many challenges and expectations. By all accounts it was a loving marriage and unlike many noblemen, Henry remained faithful to her throughout their time together. But just as Elizabeth was adjusting to a new life, so was Henry. He had spent so much of his life in exile that he had formed his suspicious character. He would never trust anyone other than his own instincts, and probably his mother and Uncle Jasper. Elizabeth had to accept that she would have limited power when it came to influencing her husband in matters of governance.

During the early years of his reign Henry had to teach himself to be more accepting of Elizabeth's lineage, he was ever-wary of her Yorkist links and was always on the lookout for any potential threat. The couple spent a lot of time together and were often found to be enjoying each other's company. They would travel together between residences and would often attend to official duties as a couple. Henry was very generous to his wife, gifts included jewels and fabric to make fine dresses but that was not to say he lavished money on her endlessly, he had his limits. But as time went on he learned to trust his wife; she would intercede with Henry whenever she felt it was necessary but this would always have been done in a private setting.

There were never any reports of Elizabeth and Henry having public disputes or having crossed words with each other. Elizabeth knew her place and what was expected of her, in public she supported her husband no matter what was being debated. From Henry's perspective, he seemed to appreciate her views and would take on board what she said. From early on in the marriage there seems to have been a mutual respect between the couple but unfortunately it was not often she managed to change his mind.

Elizabeth was everything a queen ought to be. She was beautiful, devout and kind in her nature, her personality made her very popular with the people and she would be cheered wherever she went. Queen Elizabeth definitely came from the same mould as her father, like him she had the common touch and enjoyed being among the people and took pleasure from the joy it gave them. Elizabeth was a generous queen and would often provide money for those most in need, she did this despite not having access to large funds herself. Henry may have provided her with the trappings to look and behave like a queen but with his tenuous claim to the throne, the king felt the need to give off the impression that he was strong and powerful and to him appearances of grandeur and the projection of majesty were important and he extended this to his wife. Providing funds to make Elizabeth's queenship look the part was one thing but he was not willing to provide funds for her charitable donations. Not being someone who would turn her back on someone in need, Elizabeth often dug into her own purse to help disadvantaged children, those in debtors prison and those who had formerly worked in the royal household of her father which led to her experiencing money worries of her own. But it was clear to everybody that she was a well-beloved queen and many of those she helped would often send her thank you gifts as a way of showing their appreciation. The poorer people would send her gifts of food such as fruit, cheese and sometime cakes and all were warmly received.

The reign of King Richard III brought a time of instability to the monarchy, there were a lot of scandals and rumours abound during that time that he was never really allowed to rule to the best of his ability. With his defeat at the Battle of Bosworth came an opportunity to relaunch the monarchy under the name of Tudor and Elizabeth was the open, kind and generous face of the new look royal family of England. Henry was kind to his people too but he chose do it quietly, he cared for his people but he chose to let Elizabeth take the plaudits but this did nothing for his own lasting reputation. The perception down the centuries people have of Henry VII was that he was miserly and a penny pincher. To some degree this is true, there is no denying he was careful with money but it is unfair to paint him as a man who controlled the purse strings with such venom especially when his court was considered to be one of the grandest in Europe. Henry VII picked up the baton from his father-in-law and based his court on the Burgundian royal house which meant there was to be a grand display of jewels, plate, wall tapestries and luxurious furnishings. He also promoted learning, he himself was a learned man and encouraged this at his court along with music and pageantry.

The display of grandeur and wealth was important to Henry and he displayed this through the magnificence of his court. He hoped to create the grandest court in Europe and wanted the world to see his kingship and majesty, in the hope it would banish any lingering doubts that he was not the rightful monarch of England. His court was well respected and admired right across the continent which brought him wide spread respect and opened up new channels of communication with other courts.

Both Henry and Elizabeth enjoyed hunting and they would often put on hunts across their residences for the nobility to come and enjoy. Despite all the fun and opulence of the court it was also a place for religious devotion and decorum and became a centre for learning. Musicians, scholars and the clergy all converged on Henry's court, its reputation having spread across Europe. Elizabeth was keen on music and had her own troupe of minstrels who would come to entertain her and her ladies whenever she had guests.

As well as being a place of grandeur and learning. Henry's court was the centre of the country's government, it was the place the country of England was run from. The Privy Council sat where ever Henry had his court at the time, he would set up offices in which to work from, the workaholic king very rarely took time away from the job. As a king he liked to be involved in all the decision making, he was not the kind of man who delegated tasks to his councillors and all final decisions were his and his alone.

Elizabeth had her own apartments in which she could meet with those seeking her assistance or patronage. The king and queen had corresponding apartments, each palace would include a great chamber, a presence chamber and a privy chamber, the closer you got to the privy chamber the more important you were. Henry knew that wealth meant power and if you had power as a king it meant you sat securely on your throne. He raised his money through taxes, by understanding wealth equals power, he realised that he needed the people to remain relatively poor. He did not want the rich getting richer as it could lead to a possible revolt against his kingship. The raising of taxes made him unpopular which bothered him not one jot.

He was also not bothered what people thought when he took the inheritance of Elizabeth's sisters. The York princesses had been left a share of the lands and rents from the Earls of March and Clare. It was an inheritance that came down through the York line but he took it all from them, leaving the York princesses with no dowries when they married, making them a less attractive option for a man of high rank. There is no evidence to suggest Elizabeth intervened on behalf of her sisters but it seems unlikely that she would not have had a word with Henry over something as personal as the York inheritance. If she did try to intervene she was sadly unsuccessful. The reluctance to hand out his money affected his wife too as it took time for Elizabeth to receive her full marriage allowance. But Henry was realigning his assets and the queen eventually received the March and Clare lands along with those of her mothers and when her grandmother died she received all the taxes and rents from her too, which were hers by right.

It would appear Henry purposely left Elizabeth short of funds meaning she was always dependent on him but what it did do was force her to take out loans from her sisters and sometimes embarrassingly for the queen, from her servants. Elizabeth amassed debts that she could not settle by herself, in fact, they got so bad that she had to pawn jewels and plate to settle them in full. She did turn to her husband for help and he willingly loaned her the amounts she needed but he would expect her to repay the debt in full to him. In fairness to Henry, he did have a lot of people to provide for, including the Queen Dowager and the unmarried York princesses and they required a certain standard of living.

Despite the money worries and Henry's ability to rub people up the wrong way his marriage to Elizabeth blossomed and it was clear they had a deep love and respect for each other. For the first time in his life Henry had a stable home life and before long the royal family was to add to its numbers. To great celebration, the queen was pregnant.

Chapter Twelve

Elizabeth, the Mother

News of the queen's pregnancy so early in the marriage would have brought great joy and happiness to the king and his court. Henry wanted to build a new royal dynasty for England and the birth of a son and heir would have made this dream possible, it would also have made him more secure on his throne. As always, Henry was looking for a way to hammer home his idea of kingship and his right to the throne through his ancestors so he decided the birth of his first child was an ideal opportunity to remind people of his ancient royal lineage. Therefore, he made the decision that his first born was to be delivered in the ancient capital of Winchester, the supposed location of King Arthur's Camelot.

We can only assume Elizabeth had very little choice in the matter, she was probably just relieved that she was able to provide an heir so early in her marriage. Of course, everyone would have been holding their breath for the birth of a son, the idea of this child being a girl would more than likely not have been openly discussed at court. The birth of a son, the first Tudor prince no less, was going to usher in a new golden age of English rule and in order to ensure peace and stability Henry needed that son fast.

The king decided the move to Winchester should take place at the end of August. It would have been quite a trek as the royal court did not travel lightly and many would have wanted to have been lodged nearby ready to congratulate the king and queen on the safe arrival of their first born. It would not have been an easy journey for an expectant Elizabeth. The roads would have been rough and bumpy and even though she would have travelled in a luxury litter decked out in plush cushions she must have been uncomfortable at times.

When she arrived in Winchester she was lodged at St Swithin's Priory which was attached to the Cathedral. It also gave her full access and use of the Prior's house and it was here she established her household but space was tight so she only brought those who were close to her including her mother, sisters and Henry's mother, Margaret Beaufort.

A first pregnancy for any woman can be an anxious time and that was no different for Queen Elizabeth and as she approached the birth she would have relied on the women around her to ease her fears and allay her worries. In preparing for the birth, it is likely Elizabeth followed the *Royal Ordinances for a Royal Birth* which had been specifically written for her by her mother-in-law Margaret Beaufort. It provides an incredibly detailed account of how Elizabeth ought to approach the birth. It mentions details such as the type of bedding sheets that should be used and what the mattress should be stuffed with, the comfort was of obvious importance to the labouring mother.

Whether Elizabeth was grateful for such strict protocol we do not know but as this was her first experience she may have felt relieved that someone had taken control, that is not to say she would follow these rules for any of her future pregnancies. Margaret was an overbearing mother-in-law and there are in fact reports that Elizabeth went against the rules and admitted a man to her presence after she had entered her confinement. No doubt this would have shocked Lady Margaret given her strict ways of doing things but sadly her reaction has not been recorded, nor can we be certain it did happen. In Elizabeth's defence the man she is supposed to have met was Francois of Luxembourg and was therefore a kinsman to Elizabeth via her grandmother.

The plans laid out for the queen would have been somewhat similar to what her mother had followed during her pregnancies, of which there were many so she certainly had experience, unlike Lady Margaret who had only ever given birth the one time. Confinement was expected to begin around four to six weeks prior to the birth, this was in part due to not being caught out whilst the queen was still performing public duties. It would not have been right and proper for the queen's waters to have broken and for her to have gone into labour in front of the court. Once her time had come, the queen would have said goodbye to the king and his court and be locked in a sealed chamber where all-natural light was shut out using thick tapestries. A fire would be blazing in the hearth, no matter the weather, and given she was giving birth in August one can only imagine the temperatures were still on the mild side. The birthing chamber was strictly a female-only area prior to the birth and only the husband would be permitted access to it afterwards unless things had gone seriously wrong and a physician may be required. This was a time when sadly knowledge of the importance of hygiene and the physical aspect of giving birth was perhaps not fully understood. The process of childbirth was very much the business of women. Elizabeth would have been attended by a female midwife and some of her closest female companions, more than likely her mother, sisters and mother-in-law were all on hand to offer support and comfort to the queen as she laboured through the night.

Prince Arthur Tudor, Duke of Cornwall was safely delivered in the early hours of the morning of 20 September 1486. Immediately following his birth, the baby prince would have been bathed, swaddled and placed in his crib. As the heir to the throne Arthur would have had two cribs, one for official means, for when people came to look on him and one for sleeping in. Naturally the king was delighted to have his son and heir and it seemed to all that the Tudor dynasty was secure at last. Henry could no longer be questioned over his eligibility to the throne, not now a male heir had been born to the queen, the rightful queen, making baby Arthur the Yorkist heir, no one would ever be able to question his right to rule when the time came.

Questions have been raised over Arthur's birth given that he was born eight months after his parents were married but that is of course if he was born full term. If he was, then he must have been conceived sometime between 29 December and 6 January, but Henry and Elizabeth did not marry until 18 January. If we accept that he was born on or around his due date then the union between his parents must have been consummated prior to their marriage ceremony in the January but that is not as scandalous as it sounds. Once the pre-contract was agreed it was acceptable for the couple to begin sleeping with each other as in the eyes of the law and God they were technically married. Some historians have commented that Henry was concerned by the rumours that Elizabeth and her uncle Richard had been intimate with each other and the king wanted to know for certain if she was a virgin prior to him marrying her. This is of course a preposterous accusation to make given that we know the talk between the couple about marrying was false. Also, given what we know of Elizabeth's character and reputation renders this a non-starter in terms of the rumour mill. The more likely and simple explanation is baby Arthur just didn't arrive on his due date.

Like most babies, Arthur could have been born a month early and there is some evidence to support this theory. It has been well documented that he was born a weak child who needed some kind of specialist care almost immediately following his birth. So much so, a special household was set up at Farnham to take care of the prince for the first six months of his life. It was decided that he needed to be carefully looked after and would not have been strong enough to make the whole journey back to London. Elizabeth Darcy was chosen, presumably by Elizabeth, to tend for Arthur. She had been Elizabeth's own nurse along with her brothers and sisters and so she must have had complete faith in her to look after her precious child in the first few months of his life.

When news of his birth was announced the cathedral bells were rung and a *Te Deum* was sung in churches across the country. At four days old Prince Arthur was christened, it was not unusual to christen a baby so soon after birth, it did not always indicate there was a health concern but infant mortality was high and it ensured the babe did not get caught in purgatory, it would have guaranteed him a place in heaven should the very worst happen. Customs dictate that Elizabeth and Henry would not have attended the ceremony, this was Arthur's moment. He would have had his godparents on hand to see to his needs during the ceremony. Dressed in a mantle of crimson cloth of gold and an ermine train, Prince Arthur was carried from the queen's chamber by her eldest sister Cecily, following behind were her sister Anne, the Marquess of Dorset and the Earl of Lincoln who bore the train. Before them went 200 torch bearers, then came many great lords and ladies of the court. When they reached the cathedral his godmother Dowager Queen Elizabeth stood waiting to greet her grandson, his godfathers were Thomas Stanley, the Earl of Derby and John de Vere, the Earl of Oxford. There was no role for his paternal grandmother Margaret Beaufort and her reaction to this is not recorded. Other members of Elizabeth's family took part in the ceremony, Lionel Woodville officiated as Bishop of Salisbury and there was a role for Margaret Clarence, Elizabeth's cousin, her brother Edward, Earl of Warwick remained in the Tower of London.

During the grand ceremony, Henry would have sat with Elizabeth in her chambers, maybe with Lady Margaret. The queen had not yet been churched and could therefore not leave her rooms but that did not prevent her being lavishly dressed for her moment of glory. When the christening party returned the baby was placed into Elizabeth's arms where he received the blessing from both of his proud parents. Then, the little baby who was the heir to the houses of Lancaster and York and a sure sign that God was pleased with union of his parents and his father's kingship was then placed in his cradle. Elizabeth was no doubt a relieved and happy mother as she became the first un-crowned Queen of England to bear a son and heir since 1066.

It is known that at birth the baby was not perhaps as strong as people would have hoped and the infant's fragile health would have been of great concern to Elizabeth and Henry. But there was more worry on the horizon when the queen fell ill with a fever shortly after the birth. It was not unusual for a woman to develop such a fever in the days following the birth, and at a time when the mortality rate for mothers following a birth was high there must have been huge anxiety all round. To everyone's huge relief Elizabeth regained her strength and was churched approximately six weeks after the birth of her son. Churching was a ceremony of purification and thanksgiving and the mother could not leave confinement until she had been blessed by a priest. Elizabeth was churched at the chapel doors where the bishop sprinkled her with holy water, she was then led into the church where a mass was said in celebration of her and the child's good health. Once she had been through the ceremony of churching, she could return to normal life and return to court. As with most noble women she left the care and upbringing of her newborn baby to an army of nurses, which was common practice at the time and was something she would have been prepared for.

But the birth left had Elizabeth feeling weak for many months and this may also add to the reasons for leaving Arthur in Farnham. Before leaving for home, Elizabeth donated a generous amount of money to the cathedral in Winchester in thanks for a safe delivery and a comfortable stay. Henry departed for London whilst Elizabeth travelled with Arthur arriving in Farnham, approximately 35 miles south west of London, on 26 October.

A household which would have been handpicked by the king and queen was already established at the bishop's palace to take care of Arthur. Elizabeth did not stay long, she left her baby in the care of the nurses and returned to London where she was reunited with Henry in Greenwich by early November. It must have been a wrench for Elizabeth having to leave Arthur at such a young age but she would visit her son as often as she could but as queen she did not have as much free time as she perhaps would have liked. Sadly, it seems Elizabeth was given little opportunity to bond with her baby, but then that was the norm with noble women, even more so with royal women as they had to return to their duty of conceiving the next, but Elizabeth would wait another two and a half years before she fell pregnant again.

The birth of Arthur had elevated the Woodvilles to high favour with the king. He created Thomas Grey, Elizabeth's half-brother, the Marquess of Dorset but that goodwill would not last or stretch to everyone, he had his limits and his actions would show no one was safe from Henry's ruthlessness. In the February the king confiscated all the property of the Dowager Queen Elizabeth, she was instead to be granted a pension of 400 marks which were to be paid in installments. The reasons for him doing this are a little murky as up to this point he seemed perfectly content with Elizabeth's mother being a part of his court, he did after all reinstate her to her former standing. So what were the reasons for Henry's actions? At the time the explanation given was that this was in punishment for the dowager queen having made peace with Richard III back in 1484. This seems like a very strange course of action to take given Henry already knew of this before he became king and married her daughter. But now that Elizabeth had given him a son did he feel she no longer needed her mother, was he simply tolerating the former queen whilst his wife settled into her role of wife and queen?

One other explanation could be that he thought her to be in someway in a plot to remove him from the throne and replace him with the Earl of Warwick. But again this makes no sense at all, why would she want Warwick, the son of her one-time enemy Clarence, on the throne when her daughter was queen and her grandson a future king. Unsurprisingly there is no evidence to back this claim up either and in reality can be utterly dismissed as being fantasy.

Knowing what we know of Henry's character and his economical capabilities it looks like nothing more than a reason to take her lands and money from her and place them elsewhere. Although to be fair to Henry he could probably no longer afford to support two queens and his mother who in all fairness lived like a queen. Supporting three great ladies and their households would not have come cheap and as his queen, Elizabeth required the biggest and most efficient household and that cost money. So, the extra revenue he got from Elizabeth Woodville's rents he arranged to be transferred to her daughter Elizabeth to help with her mounting household costs so he certainly was not siphoning the cash away to boost his own coffers.

Following the loss of her income, the dowager queen was left with no choice but retire to St Saviour's Abbey in Bermondsey which stood just across the river from the Tower of London. There were plenty of religious houses she could have moved to but thankfully for Elizabeth, she was within easy reach should she need her. Now that Henry had spare funds, he finally paid Elizabeth her dowry but the extra money left a bitter taste for Elizabeth knowing her mother was now going without the comforts she had grown used to. We can only assume that Elizabeth tried to talk Henry out of this plan but she appears to have been unable to intercede on behalf of her mother and this whole affair would have caused her great upset. It seems rather cold and callous but Henry expected the extra money to pay Elizabeth's debts which were a growing concern for him. To those on the outside it appears that he is punishing the mother for the sins of the daughter and fixing the problem of Elizabeth's debts didn't cost him a penny.

Money was of no concern when it came to organising Elizabeth's coronation and the time had come to make the necessary arrangements, Henry couldn't delay it any longer he had promised to crown Elizabeth and make her queen as part of the marriage agreement. She had given him a son and heir and it was now time for her to be rewarded. The king and queen celebrated Christmas at Greenwich but rumours had begun to circulate at court that the Earl of Warwick had somehow managed to escape from his prison cell at the Tower of London. People were gossiping that the young Earl had not been seen for some time, had Henry done the unthinkable and followed in the footsteps of Richard III and done away with the very threat to his throne? For the nervous and paranoid king, the fact there was a threat to his throne caused him to delay Elizabeth's coronation once again.

But this was not just gossip as news soon reached him there was a pretender in Ireland claiming to be the Earl of Warwick. Were the rumours true, had he managed to escape the mighty fortress and make his way overseas? If he had then he would have needed help on the outside, Henry was more than concerned but of course he knew Warwick was safely locked away where he had put him just under two years before. So, who was in Ireland claiming to be the rightful King of England? Recent studies suggest it was Edward V having escaped from the Tower but at the time the young pretender went by the name of Lambert Simnel and was being supported by

John de la Pole, Earl of Lincoln. It turned out he was the illegitimate son of an organ maker in Oxford but details surrounding Simnel are questionable, we do not know for sure of his parentage or if in fact that was his real name. what we do know is that he was a boy of 10 years old and had become a pupil of a priest named Richard Simon. Simon trained Simnel well in how to behave with proper refined manners, he gave him a good standard of education and at some point decided to pass him off as the young Earl of Warwick following rumours he had died. Unbelievably he somehow managed to convince some Yorkist supporters that Simnel was in fact Warwick and many flocked to his banner of the bear with a ragged staff. Simon took Lambert over to Ireland where the Yorkists still had a large following. He presented him the Earl of Kildare who was taken in by the story and agreed to lead an attack to invade England to remove Henry and replace him with Warwick/Simnel.

Whether his supporters truly believed Simnel was the Earl of Warwick is unknown, they may have just seen an opportunity and exploited the young boy for their own advantage but it appears many were taken in by Simnel. On the one hand that is understandable because not many people knew what the Earl of Warwick actually looked like because he had been imprisoned from such a young age, so Simon's Simnel offered a plausible story. It was so plausible that Lambert Simnel was crowned on 24 May 1487 at Christ Church Cathedral in Dublin, he took the regnal name of Edward VI.

Following the coronation, the Earl of Lincoln, one time heir of Richard III fled to Flanders in a bid to build support for his new king. He went straight to the Burgundian court where he told of the plot to free Warwick, he explained he had taken part in the escape of Warwick from the Tower. Upon hearing this, Margaret of York, Dowager Duchess of Burgundy and aunt to Lincoln and the real Warwick believed what she was told and raised 2000 men who would accompany Lincoln back to Ireland in preparation for war. Margaret hated Henry because he had killed her brother Richard, took his throne and caused the collapse of the House of York. The fact her niece

Elizabeth had married Henry to unite the two royal houses meant nothing to her, she hated Henry with a violent passion and would do anything in her power to remove him from the throne. She even accused Elizabeth of being a traitor for marrying him. Warwick was her nephew and despite having never met him (or probably having never met him) she was convinced that he was free and therefore should take his rightful place on the throne of England. In the May of 1487, the Earl of Lincoln set sail for Ireland, he had men at his back and was to pledge his allegiance to the pretender and prepare to invade England.

In order to put down the plot the only option open to Henry and his councillors was to show the real Earl of Warwick to the public. It seemed rather a straightforward response to the rebels and knowing that he could do this makes the rebel's plans dead in the water for you cannot claim to have someone in your keeping when you know your enemy has them. Warwick was taken from his prison in the Tower of London and paraded through the streets of London to St Paul's to attend mass. He was shown in a regal state as befitted his royal status but the poor boy was said to be 'unresponsive and backward. It was reported he had the mental age of a one-year-old but whilst he lived he remained a threat to Henry and therefore he must remain a prisoner of the state.

When news of the invasion reached Henry he was at the stronghold of Kenilworth Castle in the midlands. He sent instructions to the queen's chamberlain, the Earl of Ormond, that he was to escort the queen directly to Kenilworth, concerned for the welfare and safety of her child, Elizabeth headed straight for Farnham to collect Arthur before heading to Kenilworth with Margaret Beaufort reaching the king on 29 May. Elizabeth and Arthur were to stay at Kenilworth in the care of Bishop Courtenay. Then came the news that the invaders had landed on the north-west coast in Lancashire on 4 June and were marching to meet the king at Coventry. The rebel army consisted of Irish and Flemish men but were quickly joined by the few Englishmen who were still loyal to the white rose. As the invaders marched across England they found very little support for their cause and decided to re-group and make a new plan. They set up camp in a small Nottinghamshire village called East Stoke which was just ten miles from the king's forces. The two armies finally clashed at Stoke Field on 16 June. It was a long and hard-fought battle but the king was victorious. Lincoln was among the dead and Simnel was taken prisoner. Simon was pardoned but was sent to prison for life, no doubt his religious vocation saved him from a traitors death. The Earl of Kildare was also pardoned based on the fact he had remained in Ireland, clearly not willing to get his hands dirty.

Many pleaded for mercy and were pardoned but what of the 10 year old Lambert Simnel? The pretender to Henry's throne would surely be punished for thinking he could usurp the throne. Surprisingly the king was very lenient on him and he was set to work in the royal kitchens where he worked hard for his new royal master. He impressed the king so much that he would later rise high within the royal household. His life once he entered royal service becomes blurred but it is believed he married and had children and died at some point after 1534. The forgiveness and promotion of Lambert Simnel is a prime example of Henry VII's kind nature. The king may have had to go to war to defend his throne but he clearly understood that a 10-year-old boy was nothing but a puppet for those desperate for revenge and power. Henry was not a vengeful person and by forgiving Lambert he gained a valued member of the royal household.

Henry was showing himself to be a more than competent king on the battlefield, triumphant in battle once more, he returned to Kenilworth having successfully defended his realm. As he approached Kenilworth he knew waiting for him was a relieved Elizabeth and a baby Prince Arthur who had no idea what his father had gone through to protect his inheritance. It would seem the Tudor dynasty was here to stay and now the pretender had been dealt with it was Elizabeth's time to shine.

Chapter Thirteen

Elizabeth, the Queen

With a sense of security, Henry made sure the crowning of his wife was delayed no longer and he spared no expense on her special day. The royal couple returned victoriously to London from Kenilworth with Henry entering his capital city to huge acclaim. Looking proudly on from the windows of the Hospital of St Mary Spital in Bishopsgate were Elizabeth and his mother who were joined by the great lords and ladies of the court. A great service of thanksgiving was given at St Paul's and from there the royal party moved to Greenwich to take stock of the events over the past few weeks and to prepare Elizabeth for her big day.

On 23 November Elizabeth left Greenwich accompanied by her mother-in-law and a group of specially selected lords and ladies from the court. The royal party boarded a flotilla of barges and the one that belonged to the students of Lincoln's Inn had been decorated with a large red dragon that breathed fire into the water. No doubt this was a nod to Henry's Welsh Tudor roots and something that caused great enjoyment as they sailed upstream to the Tower of London.

Like so many kings and queens before her Elizabeth would spend the night before her coronation at the historic fortress. To entertain the special guests as they made their way along the river, pageants were performed and as she sailed passed Elizabeth was greeted by huge cheers from the riverside. She was clearly adored by the people and she would have been heartened to see so many Londoners come out to wish her well, this moment was a long time coming for many of the old Yorkist regime but finally the ever-popular and much-loved daughter of Edward IV was going to take her rightful place on the throne of England. Also, as part of the flotilla was the Mayor of London and its Sheriffs and Guildsmen, the city was well represented. Upon arriving at the Tower, Henry, who had sailed earlier, greeted his wife and queen and escorted her directly to the royal apartments which at that time were housed in the Lanthorn Tower, the home of the queen's apartments. At the time of Henry and Elizabeth's reigns the Tower of London was not viewed as a bloody place of execution that it is today, rather it was a sumptuous palace for the royal family to enjoy. In celebration of the coming day's events, Henry created fourteen new Knights of the Bath and on the evening of the 23rd a special feast was held in their honour which the king and queen both attended.

As 24 November dawned Elizabeth made her final preparations to leave the Tower and make her official state entrance into the City of London. She wore her long golden hair loose down her back and was finely dressed in a gown of white cloth of gold with an ermine trimmed train which her sister Cecily carried for her. Cecily was a constant companion and support to her sister and she rode in a carriage behind Elizabeth's with their aunt Katherine, the Duchess of Bedford. She departed the Tower in a litter pulled by eight white horses and went in procession through the streets of London to the city, from there she headed for the Palace of Westminster.

Her Coronation Day was 25 November 1487. No doubt as she was carefully dressed in her purple velvet and ermine gown her nerves began to jangle, her day had finally arrived. She had come a long way from being the scared girl in sanctuary to the young mother who stood on the threshold of true queenship. She would have been prepared for this role from a very young age, certainly when she was betrothed to the Dauphin she would have been trained by her mother and father in how to behave and what she could expect her duties to be as a queen. But she was not becoming the Queen of France, her fate lay much closer to home and even though she didn't know it at the time her union with Henry Tudor was destined to create one of England's most iconic royal families.

Her attendants for the day were again her younger sister Cecily, her aunt the Duchess of Suffolk, her cousin, Margaret of Clarence and her ever-present mother-in-law, Margaret Beaufort. Elizabeth was tall and beautiful, her skin was pale and she had striking blue eyes she looked every inch a queen. From Westminster Hall she passed through to the Abbey and down the aisle as part of a great procession with the Bishops of Ely and Winchester by her sides. The sceptre was carried by her uncle, John de la Pole, Duke of Suffolk, the rod carried by the Earl of Arundel and finally came the crown carried by Jasper Tudor, Duke of Bedford. So as not to outshine his wife on her special day, Henry watched the ceremony hidden behind a screen with his mother. The crowds gathered to witness the occasion were vast and there are reports that in a rush to cut some of the woollen carpet the queen had walked over people were crushed and killed.

As we have recently witnessed in the coronation of King Charles III the ceremony is a solemn occasion and one that is steeped in history and tradition. The church was well represented at Elizabeth's coronation with fifteen bishops and seventeen abbots in attendance. The Archbishop of Canterbury, John Morton, greeted the queen as she approached the High Altar, she then dropped to her knees in order to be anointed with the holy oil, this was done on the forehead and breast. She would not have sat in the ancient coronation chair as she was only the queen consort and that special seat is reserved for the reigning monarch only, although there would have been many in the Abbey that day that felt it was Elizabeth's right to be crowned whilst sat upon it. Next, she would have received the sceptre and rod before the crown was finally placed on her head.

Following the crowning, Mass was heard and the new queen would have given her confession and taken communion. With the ceremony now over the newly crowned queen returned to the Palace of Westminster for the coronation banquet which was held in the ancient Westminster Hall. Elizabeth sat at the high table in her crown and robes for a grand feast. It was a formal banquet and Elizabeth would have been offered each dish to try before it was passed down to her guests, there were many courses and each course would have consisted of many dishes. Once the magnificent banquet was over she would have been offered a golden goblet of Hippocras, the spicy sweet drink which marked the end of the feasting. Undoubtedly this was Elizabeth's crowning moment but her mother and younger sisters were not permitted to attend any of the celebrations which must have been a bittersweet moment for her. The former queen no doubt sat in her rooms at Bermondsey Priory distraught that she could not witness her eldest daughter be crowned.

Resplendent in her robes and adorned with the royal regalia Queen Elizabeth shone brightly but her mother Elizabeth Woodville had been purposely excluded by Henry as a punishment for her supposed treachery. We will never truly know if the dowager queen was involved in a plot to remove them from the throne but we do know is that she was cast aside and spent the rest of her days in quiet contemplation and seclusion at Bermondsey Abbey. Did Elizabeth believe the accusations against her mother? We simply do not know, but her thoughts must have gone to her as she herself now took the step her mother had all those years before when she married her father.

The coronation celebrations lasted for a number of days and the following morning the queen heard mass in St Stephen's Chapel and from there she went to the Parliament Chamber to receive more guests and their well wishes. She then went in procession with Margaret Beaufort, the Duchess of Bedford and Cecily to another grand banquet held in her honour. As with the coronation feast this consisted of many courses of fine foods but it brought to an end the celebrations, now she had to get down to the business of being a queen.

Now she was a crowned queen Elizabeth's day to day life changed, she had her own set of ministers that she appointed herself, although maybe Henry offered her some guidance. The queen's household was designed to mirror that of the king's but they were run independently from each other meaning if one was away from court the other was still able to function. The ministers were appointed to give the queen advice, administer the vast lands she held across the country and collect the rents from those lands on her behalf. In essence the queen should never be troubled by any disputes amongst her tenants and all other domestic issues.

At the head of her household were her councillors and her chamberlain, they were there to ensure the household ran smoothly. They made sure she was clothed correctly and made arrangements for any progresses she may wish to have undertaken they also oversaw the arrangements needed for any guests she wished to entertain. Even though the two households were separate they would work in collaboration with the king and his councillors but ultimately everyone was answerable to the sovereign, even Queen Elizabeth's plans had to be sanctioned by Henry. Her council would have comprised of her chamberlain, chancellor, receiver-general (the man in charge of rent collecting), secretary, attorney-general, sergeants-at-law, knights, carver, and a clerk. All these positions were there to help the queen govern correctly, they offered advice and legal services when she needed it and would meet regularly to discuss the queen's business. The most coveted position was that of queen's chamberlain and that role fell to the Earl of Ormond, Thomas Butler and it was his responsibility to make sure the queen's privy chamber ran like a well-oiled machine.

Like in today's royal family, protocol and efficiency are important and it was no different for Henry and Elizabeth. There were many facets to the queen's household and far too many roles to mention here but needless to say every aspect of Elizabeth's life was taken care of. She needn't worry about anything as there was always someone on hand to fix an issue or make sure everything met protocol.

Naturally places in her household were coveted positions, your manners had to be impeccable and your character beyond reproach but Elizabeth was a kindly woman and often added to her household when she felt she could help someone in need. In 1501 she offered the position of carver to her half-brother Arthur Plantagenet. Arthur was the illegitimate son of her father and his mistress Lucy Walters and was approximately 5 years older than her. Any bad behaviour would reflect badly on the queen so she had to be able to trust you and believe that you would be loyal to her, if you passed those tests and managed to secure a place then you were in a very comfortable position. This was especially true of the ladies as you would receive an independent salary, a pension and access to the queen on a daily basis.

For a lady of noble birth or from a wealthy family then a place at court could be of great use to your family. It could put you in a position to request favours on their behalf, to build up the family name and snare yourself a wealthy and influential husband. In total Elizabeth had thirty two ladies in her household that would wait on her, eighteen of these were noblewomen alongside her unmarried sisters (other than the youngest Bridget as she took holy orders at the age of 10 years old). As the eldest, Cecily took the role of chief lady-in-waiting although once she married William Courteney the duty fell to Anne as the next eldest. Elizabeth liked to surround herself with family because she knew she could trust them implicitly. Her cousin Elizabeth Stafford was given the position of first lady of the bedchamber which made her the highest paid of all the ladies in attendance on the queen. Never too far from the queen was her cousin, Margaret of Clarence, the two had been close since her father's execution in 1478 and a place was found in the household for her. Sadly, Margaret's brother, the Earl of Warwick did not benefit from Elizabeth's good graces as he was still languishing in the Tower, maybe the queen felt a sense of duty towards Margaret and wanted to assist her cousin in any way she could.

The role of a lady-in-waiting meant that you attended the queen on a daily basis and would accompany her in private with tasks such as waking her in the morning, helping her to wash and dress and attending to her when she used the privy. They would brush out and dress her long golden hair for the day, now she was a married woman her hair had to be hidden away from view, that was to be for the pleasure of her husband only. The women also had to be on hand during ceremonial occasions, they would help her dress in her finery and accompany her from her rooms to the great hall or to the king. All of Elizabeth's ladies would have formed close bonds with the queen and with one another, they were as close to a friend the queen could get.

The reputation of a lady-in-waiting had to be beyond reproach and any lady wanting that position had to be accomplished in dancing and singing as well as being able to play a musical instrument. They would accompany the queen when she walked in the palace gardens and would play cards and dice with her of an evening. When you served in either the king's or the queen's court you were expected to put their needs before your own, if you were good at your job you could find yourself in that role for many years with very advantageous perks.

The rank under the ladies-in-waiting was the maid of honour. These were unmarried girls from wealthy families that were aspiring to become members of the queen's inner sanctum when they got older. Again, their character had to be impeccable and they had to be educated in all the accomplishments that befitted the rank of Lady. It was a lucrative position and competition was high to get a place at court. Wealthy families would look to place their daughters in a decent position to win a spot at court and some would even go as far as placing them in the beds of wealthy courtiers. Ordinarily, recommendations often came via a lady-in-waiting and once you were there your family's reputation depended on your remaining free of scandal and keeping favour with the queen.

Being a member of the queen's household meant you had to look the part and members would be requested to wear the queen's livery. They were expected to be well turned out but never as well dressed as the queen herself and the sumptuary laws were brought in to ensure this never happened. Henry understood the need to appear well dressed and to look regal and he made sure Elizabeth and her household had funds available in order for her to dress as a queen should.

As well as looking the part a queen's biggest duty was to provide heirs for her husband. Prince Arthur was growing up to be stronger than many thought he would, given his delicate nature at birth but the Spanish ambassador Rodrigo de Puebla commented that at the age of two the young prince had 'so many excellent qualities'. With his reign in its relative infancy Henry looked to strengthen his relations overseas and he looked towards Spain to make a marriage between Prince Arthur and the daughter of Ferdinand of Aragon and Isabella of Castille, Infanta Katherine. Despite the young ages of the bride and groom the prospect of a potential marriage was first discussed in March 1488 and if it came off it would be a huge coup for Henry but it would take until March the next year for the details to be agreed upon. It was an important match for England as it was an opportunity to cement themselves amongst Europe's powerful elite, it would open up vital trade links but more importantly it would be a clear signal that Henry was the accepted and undisputed king of England. The marriage came as part of the Treaty of Medina del Campo which stipulated the infanta's dowry would consist of 200,000 crowns, the deal was ratified on 23 September 1490 but it would be many years before the young couple would wed.

With the future of her eldest child seemingly settled Elizabeth entered confinement for the birth of her second child at Westminster on 31 October 1489. Her confinement would have followed a similar pattern as before, she would have said goodbye to the court, and to Henry, and sealed herself away with her women. Her daughter was born safely on 28 November 1489, she was named Margaret for her grandmother. By the November of 1490, the queen told her husband she was pregnant again and on 28 June 1491 Elizabeth gave birth to her second son Henry at the Palace of Placentia in Greenwich. He was a robust baby with red hair, he was said to resemble his grandfather Edward IV and that was a comparison that would continue be made as the prince grew into a man.

Prince Henry was given his own household at Eltham Palace and as more children were added to the royal nursery this palace in Kent became the premier residence for the royal children. The birth of a second son gave Henry VII his spare heir yet as his rule was challenged once more by another pretender having two Tudor sons in the royal nursery was even more important.

Chapter Fourteen

A Second Pretender

In the autumn of 1491 Ireland was once again the focus of a plot to overthrow Henry VII by the way of a pretender called Perkin Warbeck and this time the threat was far more serious than that of Lambert Simnel. Warbeck was a 16-year-old lad and he announced that he was in fact, Prince Richard, the Duke of York and the younger brother of Edward V, and of Queen Elizabeth. The reports received by Henry suggested the young pretender resembled Edward IV and could possibly have been an illegitimate son of the former king, either way he posed a threat to Elizabeth's husband and their children. But if it was the Duke of York, how had he managed to escape from the Tower?

There have been many rumours put about that both boys were spirited away from the Tower under the cover of darkness and smuggled abroad for safety. But there were also suggestions that Richard's mother had somehow managed to smuggle him out of sanctuary and exchange him for a boy of a similar age and looks. She was well aware that Richard III would come for her second son and she had support within the confines of sanctuary that would have helped to arrange a safe passage out of Westminster and to safety.

It was said the young prince had been sent into the service of a staunch Yorkist supporter named Sir Edward Brampton who fled to the Netherlands after the Battle of Bosworth. Brampton was a godson of Edward IV so would have been loyal to his widow and children and the suggestion was that he fled to the court of Margaret of Burgundy and it is believed he met the young Perkin Warbeck here. This version of events does fit in very well with the rumours but if Brampton had spirited away the real Prince Richard of York then there would be no need to use Warbeck in an attempt to oust Henry, surely he could come and claim the throne in his own name. The idea of one of the princes managing to flee the country is not widely accepted, the princes either died together in the Tower of London or they were taken from there to a place of safety within England, somewhere that Richard could keep them safe but contained. But as mentioned earlier new evidence has come to light that may cast doubt on everything we think we know about the two boys and their fates.

Many believed the young pretender was a protégé of Margaret of Burgundy and that this was another attempt of hers to unseat her hated rival. Margaret was proving to be a constant thorn in Henry's side and Brampton is said to have placed the boy with the duchess after she became intrigued when she heard the comments about his likeness to her brother. Warbeck announced himself to be Richard Duke of York and the younger brother of King Edward V at Margaret's Burgundian court in 1490. He told people that his brother had been murdered but he had been spared given his young age (he was 9 years old). He managed to make his way to Europe with the help of loyalist Yorkist supporters, his main keeper had been Brampton, and they had kept him safely hidden for seven years. After some reflection Margaret decided to believe that he was her nephew and that everything he had recounted had been a true account of the prince's story. She decided to send the boy to the Yorkist supporters in Ireland in the hope they would help to stir up trouble, he set sail in 1491 for Ireland where he immediately gained the backing of John Atwater, the Mayor of Cork. Support for Warbeck did not materialise any further than Cork and he was forced to return to Margaret.

After the Lambert Simnel incident Henry was well aware just how much his rival in Burgundy hated him and so took the threat seriously. To the king of England this was no young boy pretender, this was a young man with a credible back story and does the way Henry treated the threat prove to us that he genuinely had no idea what had happened the Princes in the Tower?

The anguish that Elizabeth must have felt throughout this time must have been a torment to her. She, like everyone else, never actually knew what had happened to her younger brothers and for seven years had learnt to live with the knowledge that no one could tell her what exactly became of them. But things were different now, gone was the young girl in sanctuary who missed her little brothers, who watched her anguished mother tear at her hair in sheer desperation. Instead, now she was a queen, a wife and most importantly of all, a mother and a mother to a future king of England at that. The chances that the interloper who went by the name of Perkin Warbeck was in fact the Duke of York were very slim as there were inconsistences in his back story but for many of the elder Yorkist supporters it didn't matter for they were willing to believe and support Perkin Warbeck.

After Warbeck returned from Ireland he was sent to the court of King Charles VIII of France where he was welcomed with open arms in fact, he welcomed him as a king, King Richard IV of England! He was given royal apartments and shown every courtesy a king could expect. But sadly, for Warbeck it was not to last, Henry sailed to France to discuss peace terms and on 3 November 1492 a peace treaty was signed between the two countries. The Treaty of Étaples ensured the English army that had laid siege to Boulogne in October in retaliation to the French support of Warbeck would be ended and in return the French would cease any support for Warbeck. It didn't come cheap for Henry though as he had to rescind Brittany to French control but in return received a monetary payment to compensate for any loss.

The signing of this treaty was a show of English strength and power, in managing to force France to seek peace shows a true fear of English retaliation. It also removed Warbeck from France as it drove the pretender out of France and back to Burgundy where Henry's attention now turned. He petitioned Philip, Duke of Burgundy over his support of a known pretender, when no response came he imposed a trade ban on the duchy which not only punished the Burgundians but the English traders too. When Warbeck arrived, his 'aunt' Margaret publicly declared him her nephew, Richard, Duke of York. He was given a magnificent house in Antwerp and was again treated like a king; he even had his own court which he kept under the royal arms of England. The Warbeck roadshow continued to gain support when he was accepted as Richard IV by the Holy Roman Emperor Maximilian I.

Whilst Warbeck was safely ensconced in Antwerp playing at being King Richard, life went on at the English court. Sadly, the Queen Dowager passed away at Bermondsey Abbey on 8 June 1492, she was buried next to her husband Edward IV at St George's Chapel, Windsor. Elizabeth was unable to be with her mother as she breathed her last as she was about to enter confinement with her fourth pregnancy at Sheen where on 2 July 1492 she safely delivered a second daughter, Elizabeth. When she was old enough, the infant princess went to join her elder brothers and sister in the royal nursey at Eltham.

The royal siblings were soon to be split as Prince Arthur, at the age of six, was sent to Ludlow Castle to establish his own household. It was important that the Prince of Wales learnt how to govern and he would be taught all the necessary skills needed for kingship here. It was also a great piece of propaganda as it was Henry's way of showing his people he had his heir and no pretender could shatter the Tudor dynasty.

Once he was installed at Ludlow, Arthur would preside over the council of the Marches and Wales. He was given loyal and reliable men as members of his council which was headed up by his great uncle Jasper Tudor, the Duke of Bedford, his great-uncle Thomas Grey, the Marquess of Dorset, Thomas FitzAlan, the Earl of Arundel, Gerald FitzGerald, the Earl of Kildare, Sir William Stanley and John Alcock, Bishop of Worcester. Arthur would rely on these men to guide him through the tricky path of learning to rule and in early 1493 he also added Sir Richard Pole to his household as his Chamberlain and Dr John Argentine as his physician. There were other members of the council and household too including Arthur's tutors who helped develop the prince into a studious young man. But it was important that Arthur had someone of a similar age to interact with so Gruffydd ap Rhys ap Thomas was brought to Ludlow and the two boys formed a strong friendship.

With Arthur now settled in Ludlow, Elizabeth had to adjust to life being parted from one of her children which could not have been easy for her. Once she had bid her shy little prince goodbye she knew she would only see him on special occasions such as high feast days and Christmas, but at least she knew he was safe and out of harm's way. With the eldest son away ruling his own lands the time came for Prince Henry to have titles bestowed on him. the young Prince had many titles conferred on him as the second son of the monarch including at just ten months old when he was created Lord Warden of the Cinque Ports, Constable of Dover Castle and Earl Marshal of England which would have provided an income for him and then just a year later he was created the Lord Lieutenant of Ireland and Warden of the Scottish Marches, again, all would generate income for him which his father would be able to control.

The most covetous title for Henry came in October 1494 at the age of 3 years old when he was created the Duke of York at Westminster Palace. It is often the case that the second son of the monarch is bestowed this title but in this case it was also done in defiance to the pretender Perkin Warbeck who claimed to be the true Duke. Warbeck was still in Antwerp no doubt plotting his attack on England when information reached Henry that Warbeck was in fact the son of a boatman from Tournai but whether his intelligence could be trusted was another matter. The possible invasion led by Warbeck was playing on Henry's mind but he had to bide his time and be patient what he didn't want to do was make the first move and get it wrong, he needed to see how the land lay at home in England before striking at his enemy.

The year of 1495 got off to a busy start for the king and queen, in the March Elizabeth was given the castle, manor and town of Fotheringhay a place with strong Yorkist links to the queen's past which would have increased her much depleted revenues. By April the king bestowed his favour even further by naming his queen as the Chief Lady of the Garter, he also made the young Prince Henry a Knight of the Garter. Sadly, in the May, Elizabeth's grandmother,

Cecily Neville, the Dowager Duchess of York passed away at the grand age of 80 at Berkhamsted Castle in Hertfordshire. She had been known as the 'Rose of Raby' when she was younger and had married her true love, Richard Plantagenet at the age of 8, they had twelve children together. She saw two of her sons crowned king of England and also saw one of them execute the other. With her death Elizabeth gained the Yorkist stronghold of Baynard's Castle and the revenues from her estates which passed to her as her next of kin.

On 1 July the king and queen set out on their annual summer progress, this year they decided to travel north, visiting Arthur at Ludlow on the way. Their destination was Lancashire, the home county of Thomas Stanley, Earl of Derby, he greeted them and escorted them to his estates at Lathom House in Ormskirk. Lathom had been the seat of the Stanleys since the late twelfth-century and stood in its own deer park overlooking the small town of Burscough and the marsh land of Martin Mere. The royal couple stayed at Lathom for four days as guests of Lord Derby and his wife, Henry's mother Margaret Beaufort.

Whilst the royal couple was away Warbeck made his attempt to invade England. Funded by Margaret of Burgundy he landed at Deal in Kent on 3 July, he had with him fourteen ships but the king's forces dealt with them and the pretender fled to Ireland but the Irish had already declared they had no interest in supporting Warbeck. When he arrived at Cork he was denied entry so he had no option but to sail up to Scotland in the hope he would receive a better welcome from England's auld enemy north of the border. On 3 August Henry and Elizabeth travelled to Derby's hunting lodge, Knowsley which sits east of the city of Liverpool, from there they turned southwards and visited Manchester before arriving in the midlands at Stafford. They were finally back at Sheen on 3 October, they were not home long before tragedy hit.

On 7 October 1495 news reached Henry and Elizabeth their 3-year-old daughter princess Elizabeth had died at Eltham Palace. It would appear that her death was sudden given the fact her parents had stopped at Sheen and made no attempts to rush to see their daughter. In fact, the king was in negotiations with France to marry her to Francois, the future king of France so it appears she was not a sickly child and was certainly not expected to die so young. The princess was brought from Eltham to Westminster Abbey, her little coffin was laid on a chariot which was pulled by six horses to the gates of Westminster Abbey where it was received by the prior. The funeral took place on 26 November with great ceremony, as was customary for the time the king and queen did not attend their daughter's funeral. A small marble tomb was erected where the young girl was laid to rest. The tomb stands close to the tomb of King Henry III but has since been moved. The inscription on the side of the tomb read:

> Elizabeth, second child of Henry the Seventh King of England, France and Ireland and of the most serene lady Queen Elizabeth his consort, who was born on the second day of the month of July in the year of Our Lord 1492, and died on the fourteenth day of the month of September in the year of our Lord 1495, upon whose soul may God have mercy. Amen
>
> Here, after death, lies in this tomb a descendent of royalty, the young and noble Elizabeth, an illustrious princess. Atropos, most merciless messenger of death, snatched her away. May she inherit eternal life in Heaven!

Sadly, infant mortality at this time was common, there were no antibiotics or medically approved medicines available and when illness struck it often meant death, even in royal nurseries. The death of Elizabeth must have been difficult for the queen, she had to endure the loss of Arthur to Ludlow and now the loss of Elizabeth all whilst she was five months pregnant making it a very worrying time for her own health. Elizabeth was the first of Henry and Elizabeth's children to die, maybe there was an element of guilt too given they had been away from their children for three months. They were used to not living with their children, royal children did not often reside in the same royal establishment as their parents but Elizabeth especially made every effort to see her children when she could and the three-month separation must have been difficult for her. Now compounded by the loss of their daughter the king and queen grieved quietly for their loss.

Sadly, Henry and Elizabeth did not have long to grieve before news reached them that Warbeck had been received in Scotland as King Richard IV of England. King James IV had greeted Warbeck at Stirling where he presented him with clothes befitting a king, he also offered him a pension. Did James truly believe Warbeck was Prince Richard or was he simply looking for an opportunity to cause his neighbour to the south trouble? During his stay in Scotland Warbeck married. His bride was Katherine Gordon, daughter of the Earl of Huntly. The more Henry heard of Warbeck's integration into the Scottish nobility the more he became concerned and the news was spreading fast that his throne was under threat. The news had even reached Spain where Ferdinand and Isabella were starting to have doubts over the marriage between their daughter, Infanta Katherine and Prince Arthur. If Henry did not nip this rebellion in the bud he stood to lose more than a foreign marriage alliance, his whole reign as king could come crashing down leaving him, Elizabeth and their children vulnerable to their enemies.

The year of 1495 was a mixed one for Henry and Elizabeth, they had endured the loss and burial of their daughter to illness and the throne was under threat from a pretender that other countries saw as the rightful king of England. But it did see a successful progress to the north and the marriages of Elizabeth's sisters Anne and Katherine. Princess Anne married Lord Thomas Howard, son of the Earl of Surrey who would later become the 3rd Duke of Norfolk. She saw the Howards as being a noble family of old and it would be beneficial to keep them close to the throne. The queen discussed the marriage with her sister but in the end decided it was a grand match and the wedding should go ahead.

The couple married in February at Westminster Abbey with the celebrations taking place at the Palace of Placentia. Edward

IV had left a dowry of 10,000 marks but Henry never handed this over. Elizabeth instead arranged for an annuity payment of £120 to be paid to the couple per year, or until Anne's death which came in November 1511 when she was just 36 years old. By all accounts it was an unhappy marriage, Thomas had extra-marital affairs and all their children pre-deceased her. Princess Katherine was married to Lord William Courtenay, son and heir of the Earl of Devon. The couple spent much time at court and had three children together, Henry, Edward and Margaret, although Edward would die in infancy. Elizabeth approved both of these matches and contributed financially to both couples. Having such an extended family meant Henry could make powerful and advantageous matches for his sisters-in-law and both Courtenay and Howard were ardent supporters of his. Once she had seen her sister well married the time came for Elizabeth to enter back in to confinement to deliver her fifth child.

Chapter Fifteen

Victory Again

On 18 March 1496 Elizabeth safely delivered a daughter called Mary at Sheen Palace. The little princess was described as being as beautiful as her mother and she soon joined her elder brother and sister at Eltham. Before long plans were being made for the summer progress into the west country, it must have been an anxious time for Elizabeth given the last time she left her children to go on progress the toddler Elizabeth died, with a baby now in the nursery it must have been a wrench to leave her.

Elizabeth knew her duty and left Sheen with Henry on 14 July and headed for Chertsey; from there they visited Guildford before travelling further south to Southampton. They stayed briefly at Beaulieu Abbey before sailing across the Solent to the Isle of Wight. Back on the mainland their trip included visits to Poole and Corfe Castle and by 5 August they were at Salisbury. They then went on to Bath and Bristol before finally heading to Cirencester and then back on to Windsor Castle. They wouldn't have been too far from Ludlow and more than likely went to see Prince Arthur; Henry would have been interested to see how his eldest son was adapting to life at the head of his own household and how well was learning the rules of kingship, for Elizabeth it was an opportunity to be reunited with her first born and to enjoy his company.

Back home, Elizabeth's thoughts would have immediately turned to her children at Eltham and how quickly she could visit them. She often went to see them and was as hands on with her children's upbringing as a queen could be. The nursery was a female dominated environment and no doubt Prince Henry felt outnumbered at times with two sisters and nurses gushing over him. The queen took a great interest in her children's education and may have even sat with them on her lap teaching them their earliest lessons in reading, writing and learning their prayers. Following the birth of Arthur, Elizabeth had an enforced separation from him and it has been suggested that her bond with him was perhaps not as strong as it could have been. But as the heir, Arthur was by the very nature of his future role somewhat disconnected from his parents and siblings but with her younger children it was different, especially with Henry who was by all accounts her favourite.

In view of her relationship with Arthur, she made sure she engaged more with her younger children and forged close relationships with them. With Arthur settled in Ludlow the time had come for his younger brother Prince Henry to begin his formal education and the role of tutor had been assigned to the Cambridge educated John Skelton who moved to Eltham as part of his role. He was very encouraging to young Henry, he helped him to learn how to play the lute and it would transpire the prince had a talent for music. Henry was a little boy who was full of energy, a real live wire who was a keen and eager student. He liked to learn and Skelton liked to teach and the pair had a great relationship and as the prince grew older he would learn subjects like Latin, languages and classics. The princesses would also have had some kind of education and from reports it has been suggested that Margaret was more than capable of reading and writing and she had a love of dancing and music, Elizabeth encouraged her daughters to learn just as much as her sons, just as she had been by her father.

With the children happily ensconced in the royal nursery at Eltham the problem of Perkin Warbeck refused to go away, in September 1496 James IV planned to invade England with Warbeck at his side. If they were successful, Warbeck promised James that he would restore the town of Berwick back to Scotland when he took the throne but all James was interested in was a border raid to fill his coffers. The king of Scotland probably knew Warbeck was a lost cause and never truly believed he was who he said he was and he quickly retreated back over the border when the English army drew closer, but before Henry could see to his Scottish problem the king had another matter to attend to.

In order to fund his army Henry was left with no option but to raise taxes but this angered many, especially the Cornish and they marched on London to confront the king. Elizabeth was at Sheen with Henry as the protestors drew close, the king left his wife there and prepared to confront his people himself face to face. Before he left, he arranged for an escort to come and collect the queen, from there she was to go straight to Eltham to collect the children and from there she was to go to Margaret Beaufort at Coldharbour where they stayed a week before retreating to the safety of the Tower of London. The protestors plan was to enter the City of London and head straight for the Tower, they thought the king was in residence there when really he was at Lambeth Palace where he was happy to play the waiting game. It proved to be a master stroke, the rebels were exhausted after their long trek from the west country and the people of London were ready to defend their city and their royal family.

Elizabeth and the children were trapped in the Tower of London and desperate to protect his wife and children, Henry sent troops to finally quash the rebel threat. He led his own army from the front, confident that he had the people of London at his back. The two forces met at Blackheath and once again Henry came out victorious. Sadly 2000 Cornish men lost their lives that day, but yet again the king returned to London a hero. He did not celebrate for too long though, as he went straight to the Tower to see Elizabeth and the children, to reassure them all was safe and that he had been victorious in battle. Now all that remained was the problem of Perkin Warbeck, the constant niggle that chipped away at Henry.

With the Cornish threat dealt with Henry turned his attentions back to Scotland and decided to send an envoy north to enter in to discussions with King James. Henry sent men north requesting the king surrender Warbeck and to broker a peace deal but James was not for entering into these discussions, he had not had all his fun yet.

Instead, he sent Warbeck south on one of his ships with the aim of attacking the south west coast of England. Beleaguered from their failed attack on London, James may have thought it to be England's weak spot. But enroute, Warbeck decided to put in at Cork to rally support for the enterprise with Scotland but was once again refused entry to Ireland and chased away. The pretender was clearly not accepting that Ireland was not interested in supporting his cause. The delay of going via Ireland put the whole plan of attack at risk because the point of the exercise was to create a co-ordinated attack on England.

Whilst Warbeck attacked the Cornish coast, James was to go over the border, the simultaneous attack was devised to split Henry's forces but in truth his border forces were more than capable of dealing with anything James had to throw at them as border raids were commonplace and were put often down. Warbeck's impromptu visit to Ireland was not part of the plan so it put the timings of the joint attack out, and because of his delay the plan lay in ruins. It is clear that Warbeck had no military or common sense, given that he was supposedly fighting for his brother's lost crown he does not seem to have any true understanding as to how things worked. If Henry needed any further proof that Warbeck was an interloper then he needed to look no further than his capabilities of leading an army of men.

Eventually, Warbeck landed on the south west coast on 7 September 1497 at Land's End and Henry was already waiting for him. Warbeck's bride, Katherine Gordon was lodged at St Michael's Mount for safety as her husband marched his troops to Bodmin where he had himself declared King Richard IV. The Cornish were still smarting from Henry's earlier victory and may have been more inclined to support the imposter than their current king. Warbeck moved on and managed to breach Exeter but was in for a shock when the citizens repelled his attacks, this was led by Lord William Courtenay.

With trouble brewing yet again, Henry sent Elizabeth and the children into East Anglia for their safety. But whilst she was there she was to show Henry, Duke of York to the people reinforcing the fact he is the real duke and not some pretender. By all accounts, Prince Henry was an enchanting child, once that could capture the love and admiration of those around him. He was cheeky yet loveable he was boisterous and fully understood his own importance and place in the world, in essence he was the complete opposite of his elder brother Prince Arthur, and the people loved him. The plan of sending the queen and her children there was a clever move by Henry because the location of East Anglia also meant that if the trouble got too dangerous and they got backed into a corner an escape could be made by sea to the continent and safety, although Henry's track record on the battlefield would suggest an escape would not be needed.

The net was closing in on Warbeck, Henry had tracked him down to Beaulieu Abbey in Hampshire where the pretender was seeking sanctuary. Despite that, he was surrounded by the king's men and the game for 'King Richard IV' was finally up. Warbeck was taken from his sanctuary to Taunton in Somerset where he finally came face to face with King Henry. On 5 October he confessed he was not Prince Richard and that he had no right to claim the throne under that name. Henry made him write out his confession and beg for his merciful forgiveness, this was then nailed to church doors up and down the county for the people to read and to know that it had all been a lie but that their king had once again been victorious in defending his people and his crown.

With Warbeck safely imprisoned his wife Katherine Gordon was taken from St Michael's to Exeter where her husband confessed the full truth to her. Needless to say, she was distraught to learn that she had been taken in by a forgery but they were legally married and there was nothing she could do to change that. Henry took pity on the pretty Katherine and sent her to Elizabeth for her to offer her a place in her household, Henry was said to be smitten with Katherine, he paid her a pension and made sure she was well treated and not tainted by her husband's deeds. There was no evidence to suggest Henry and Katherine had an affair, in fact Henry was rare amongst noblemen in that he was faithful to his wife, there were no bastard children and no extra-marital scandals. Whether this was down to the fact he truly loved his wife and honoured her in the way he ought to or that he simply thought it was wrong we do not know, but, vows had been taken in front of God and he was determined to keep those vows sacred.

Katherine was presented to Elizabeth at Sheen on 21 October and the queen was immediately fond of her, making her a lady-in-waiting clearly the queen did not consider her a rival for her husband's affection. Katherine Gordon was of noble birth and both Henry and Elizabeth respected this and made sure she was treated as befitted her rank. Unsurprisingly, Warbeck was not treated as kindly; he was paraded through the streets of London for the people to see before being sent to the Tower of London to await his fate. Henry would have been forgiven for thinking that was the end of the matter but there were still those who believed him to be Prince Richard and claimed his confessions had been written under the threat of torture but there is no evidence to suggest he was ever mistreated whilst in custody.

So, who was Perkin Warbeck if he wasn't Prince Richard, Duke of York? By his own confession he claimed to be the son of John Osbeck, a Flemish customs controller from Tournai (in modern day Belgium) and Katherine de Faro. As a child he travelled to the Netherlands to learn how to speak Dutch, he was then taken on by a Breton merchant who first took him to Ireland, it was here that he learned to speak English. It was whilst in Cork a group of Yorkists claimed he resembled Prince Richard and that he should take on the role of the younger lost prince in the Tower in a bid to help them oust Henry from the English throne. Given his close links with Ireland it is surprising that they continually turned their backs on him whenever he went to them for help. Was it all just an elaborate joke? Did the Irish know they stood no chance of convincing others that Perkin Warbeck was in fact Prince Richard, the lost Prince in the Tower? Whatever the reason was the Irish did not want to involve themselves any further with the pretender and sent him packing each time he tried to rally support.

In a rather surprising move, Henry released Warbeck from the Tower and gave him permission to reside at court although he was to be kept under constant observation and was ordered not to leave the Palace, under any circumstances. He was reunited with Katherine and the couple became quite popular amongst those at court, it looked like the pretender had got off lightly but why would Henry treat him so well? One explanation may be that because Warbeck was not an English citizen he did not fall under English jurisdiction, Henry's hands were tied.

The court spent the Christmas of 1497 at Sheen but disaster struck when one evening a fire accidently broke out around 9pm. It is not clear whether it started in the king's or the queen's chamber but it spread quickly and destroyed much of the palace and its contents. It took three hours to get under control but when it was finally out and an assessment could be made it transpired much of the rich tapestries, plate and beds had been lost. Thankfully no one lost their life and the royal family escaped unhurt. Henry declared he was going to rebuild the palace on a much bigger and grander scale, the result of his rebuilding was Richmond Palace.

Henry's leniency of Warbeck came back to haunt him when in June 1498 he escaped from the Palace of Westminster. Managing to give his guards the slip he escaped through a window, his plan was to get to the coast and sail to the continent. Unfortunately for him he made it as far as the Charterhouse at Sheen before deciding to seek sanctuary. The prior of the Charterhouse arrived just days later to advise Henry of where Warbeck had got to, he pleaded with the king to be lenient with the young man but in fairness to Henry, he had gone down the lenient path and this was how the kindness had been repaid. Warbeck was put in the stocks on Cheapside in London and forced to read his confession aloud, from there he was taken to the Tower and there he would remain, his very being was causing problems for Henry.

The whole saga of both Lambert Simnel and Perkin Warbeck put Elizabeth in a very awkward position given that if Warbeck had been her brother her throne, and that of her husband, would potentially have been lost. But on a personal level she had lived for years in the knowledge that both her brothers had been murdered, how could she then reconcile herself if the younger brother was in fact alive and well? Henry treated Elizabeth carefully, outwardly they both commented that Warbeck was nothing but a fraud but deep down did some part of Elizabeth want this young man to be her brother? Possibly, but in all truthfulness she was likely to be relieved that he wasn't, she was a mother now and her children's interests were paramount to her.

Chapter Sixteen

A Spanish Marriage

In July 1497 an agreement had been made with Spain that Infanta Katherine would travel to England at the age of fourteen, that would be just over two and a half years away, to seal the deal. The couple were officially betrothed at Woodstock Palace in the August, Henry and Elizabeth were at the ceremony, Arthur was aged just 11 years old. The problem was that as the departure time neared for Katherine uncertainty surrounding Warbeck was a cause for concern for Ferdinand and Isabella. They were worried Henry's reign was under threat once again and that Katherine would be in danger if she sailed to England. Thankfully, the Spanish Ambassador de Puebla reassured them Warbeck was now locked in the Tower and that Infanta Katherine was safe to make her journey. Arthur's marriage was not the only one being discussed.

Henry had been in talks over the marriage of his eldest daughter Princess Margaret to King James IV of Scotland. Margaret was only 9 years old and this alarmed both Elizabeth and Margaret Beaufort, they both considered her far too young to be married off.

Their main concern was that she would be expected to travel to Scotland immediately and given that James had a reputation of being a womaniser would not wait to bed Margaret and would cause her permanent damage. Margaret Beaufort knew exactly what the dangers of being married and bedded too young could do to a girl that age. She was married to Edmund Tudor, Earl of Richmond when she was just 12 years old, Richmond was 24 at the time. He bedded Margaret straight away and she fell pregnant, she gave birth to Henry at just 13 years old. She endured a very difficult labour and it is thought that given her young age she had not fully physically matured and the birth caused her lasting damage, making her unable to bear any more children. Taking into consideration his wife and mother's pleas Henry agreed that James could not claim his bride until she reached the age of 14.

By 1499 Elizabeth was pregnant again and on 21 February she gave birth to a healthy boy at Greenwich who they called Edmund after his paternal grandfather. The infant was christened on the 24th at the Church of the Observant Friars and was styled as the Duke of Somerset from birth. Around this time Cecily's husband had died and she returned to Elizabeth's household and she may have been present in the birthing chamber when her nephew was born. By the May, Elizabeth was back at court where she and Henry observed the marriage of Prince Arthur and Infanta Katherine with de Puebla standing proxy, the ceremony took place at Tickenhill Palace in Worcestershire.

With his heir now married and with links to Spain sealed Henry could be forgiven for feeling he was now safe on his throne but no sooner had the ink dried on the marriage contract did trouble come calling. The Earl of Warwick had been in the Tower for the past fourteen years and all of a sudden his very being became a cause for concern. Ferdinand of Aragon had expressed that whilst the young man lived Katherine would not sail to England because he posed a threat to the crown. Warwick's story is a heart-breaking one, he was a young man totally innocent of any wrong-doing but the very fact he was alive was a problem for Henry, he had to die.

A plot was devised that went as follows: two gaolers named Thomas Astwood and Robert Cleymound had met Warwick in his chambers and had agreed to take control of the Tower allowing Warwick to escape and flee across the channel to Flanders where he could then launch an attack against Henry. It is highly unlikely that Warwick would be capable of understanding what they meant let alone actually carry out the plan. He had been described as being mentally young for his age, he would have no idea that what they were discussing was high treason. Two days after meeting Warwick, the same two men went to Warbeck and discussed the plot with him, he was undoubtedly keener to get involved, they told him Warwick would set him free and make him king, which was not the same plan they had relayed to Warwick. Soon enough the two men had complained that Warbeck had betrayed them and they fled into sanctuary which may suggest this was nothing short of a set-up. Another give-away to this being a manufactured plot was the close proximity in which the two prisoners had been kept, their chambers were on top of each other making it easier and believable for messages to have been passed between them. On 12 November the plot came out and by the 18th eight people were found guilty of treason at a trial held at the Guildhall. The charge was the plan to murder the Marshal of the Tower and free Warwick and Warbeck to allow them to take control, Astwood was one of those found guilty.

The day after Warwick stood trial at Westminster, he pleaded guilty to the charges and was sentenced to death, the sad thing is he more than likely had no idea what he was pleading guilty to. He was executed, like his father before him, on Tower Hill, his body was interred at Bisham Priory at the expense of Henry, he was just 24 years old. Warbeck had been arraigned on the 16 November at Westminster, the punishment for treason of a commoner was to be hung by the neck until almost dead, then cut down whilst still alive they would have their innards cut out of them and set alight in front of them. The head would then be cut off and the body hacked in to four pieces. Henry commuted this sentence to hanging alone. Perkin Warbeck was hung at Tyburn, he would have been drawn on a hurdle from the Tower to his place of execution, he swore on the scaffold that he was not the son of Edward IV.

We do not have records as to what Elizabeth felt about the execution of her helpless cousin Warwick, but knowing what we do of her character, it would have brought her great sorrow. She would probably not have had any knowledge of the plot prior to the discovery of it. Had she pleaded with her husband to spare Warwick? It would be nice to think she did but as with many decisions they were Henry's to make and Henry's alone and no amount of pleading, beseeching and tears would change his mind. In hindsight Elizabeth would have seen that the destruction of Warwick and Warbeck was a necessary evil if her son was to ever rule over a peaceful kingdom. But let us not assume Henry took pleasure from seeing these two young men executed, he did not do this to satisfy his own bloodthirsty needs, he did it to secure his throne for himself and those Tudors who came after him. Henry fell ill after the executions and took weeks to regain his strength but the executions had finally pacified Ferdinand and Isabella and confirmed Katherine would sail for England as agreed.

Safe on his throne Henry and Elizabeth travelled to Calais, they set sail from Dover and arrived on 8 May 1500. Henry had planned a meeting with Archduke Philip who incidentally was married to Katherine of Aragon's sister Juana. The meeting took place at Our Lady of St Peter's church and there was much ceremony, the church had been richly decorated and a great feast was held in honour of the two men. Over the next few days Henry and Philip had meetings to discuss the possibility of Princess Mary marrying Philip's son, Charles, a baby at just a few months old but he was the heir to the vast Hapsburg empire and Spain. Mary was only 3 years old but had already shown an early aptitude for learning and had her own household, she was described as being a beautiful child and one that greatly resembled her mother.

The royal couple stayed in Calais entertaining their guests with pageants and lavish banquets for forty days sailing home to Greenwich on 16 June. When they set foot back on English soil they were greeted with terrible news, Prince Edmund had died at aged 15 months. He had died at Hatfield, the children having been moved there for safety as the plague swept through London, it is not known what Edmund died of but we can safely say it was not the plague given there were no other deaths in the household. He was given a state funeral and buried at Westminster Abbey on 22 June. Having buried her second child, Elizabeth must have been devastated, she doted on her children and the loss of Edmund was a timely reminder that no child was safe from illness.

Good news came in October when Katherine of Aragon arrived safely on the shores of England at Plymouth, she received a rapturous reception and as she made her way to London the people cheered her. Prince Arthur met with Henry and rode out to meet Katharine on 4 November at Dogmersfield in Hampshire but things did not get off to a good start. As per Spanish custom, Katherine had to remain veiled until she was married, Henry advised her ladies they were in England now and insisted she remove her veil. Prince Arthur was very pleased as he gazed upon his wife for the first time, he left with his father and Katherine followed behind with her ladies. Elizabeth was waiting at Greenwich for them to return, Henry advised Elizabeth he was pleased with Katherine, as was Arthur, she was to be the future queen of England and had to meet his high expectations,

Elizabeth wanted her son to be happy and was thrilled to hear that the young couple seemed pleased with each other. Katherine finally arrived at Kingston-upon-Thames on 9 November where she was met by the young Prince Henry, he escorted her to Lambeth Palace where she was to lodge prior to her wedding. On 12 November Katherine made her first official entrance into London, as she arrived the church bells rung and banners were waved. There were pageants held along her route and the conduits ran with wine for the people to enjoy. This was Katherine's moment to shine, Henry, Elizabeth and Arthur watched from the windows of the Cornhill alongside many great noblemen and their ladies, who along with Margaret Beaufort waited in a nearby chamber. Her journey ended at St Paul's where she was escorted again by Prince Henry into the cathedral for a service of thanksgiving, she later returned to Lambeth Palace for the evening.

The following day Katherine went to Baynard's Castle to be officially introduced to Elizabeth, the meeting went well, using Latin as the common tongue the two women developed an instant affection for one another. Elizabeth was a kind lady and put Katherine at her ease, the two would form a strong bond and Katherine looked forward to learning all she could from Elizabeth about what it meant to be queen of England. Following Katherine's departure, Elizabeth made her way to the home of George Neville, Lord Bergavenny on Great Bartholomew Street near St Paul's where she and Henry would spend the night before the wedding.

On 14 November Prince Arthur and Katherine of Aragon married at St Paul's. Elizabeth and Henry watched the ceremony from behind a private screen as they did not want to detract from the bride and groom. Elizabeth wore a white satin gown with a purple velvet train. The wedding parties had congregated at the Tower before travelling down to the Bishop's Palace. Elizabeth travelled with Katherine in an open carriage with Henry following, wearing his red velvet robes and a diamond encrusted breastplate atop a white horse. When they arrived, they went to the Bishop's Palace, Elizabeth and Henry then privately entered St Paul's. Katherine emerged from the palace dressed in white and gold satin it was the first Spanish farthingale gown ever seen in England. She had a coronet and a voluptuous veil of silk edged with gold with her long red auburn hair flowing down her back. She was escorted to meet her groom by the ten-year-old prince Henry (Katherine's groom in 1509), Prince Arthur was also resplendent clad in white satin.

The couple were met by Henry Deane, the Archbishop of Canterbury and he was assisted by nineteen bishops and abbots. After the ceremony the newlyweds were met by huge cheers from the crowd, Prince Henry led them back to the Bishop's Palace where a lavish banquet was held. At the end of the day, the young couple were 'put to bed' in a ceremony that was witnessed by most of the guests, they were blessed as they lay in bed, the guests left and what followed was one of the most talked about wedding nights in English history.

Years later Arthur's brother, and Katherine's second husband Henry VIII, used the supposed consummation of that marriage as his get out clause from his marriage with Katherine leaving him free to marry Anne Boleyn. Canon law forbade a man to marry his brother's widow and he based his whole argument for divorce on that clause. Henry stated that God had not looked kindly on the marriage as he had not given them a living son, therefore He was angry and this was why the marriage had to be annulled. People gave varying testimonies but the only certain thing is that no one can know for certain whether or not that on their wedding night, or indeed any night after that, Katherine and Arthur consummated their marriage.

In the days following the wedding there were many tournaments, feasts and great spectacles held, special seating had been built to allow people to watch. There were dances, feasts, and pageants held at Westminster and then at Baynard's Castle, finally on 27 November the royal party sailed to Richmond for more celebrations. Prince Henry gave out special gifts to the Spanish visitors, who departed the day after. At the end of November, the family moved to Windsor and the time came for Arthur to leave and return to Ludlow, there were arguments over whether or not Katherine should join him but the king decided she must and the couple left on 21 December. Elizabeth was sad to see Arthur and Katherine leave but soon she was planning the wedding of her eldest daughter.

Chapter Seventeen

Death Strikes the House of Tudor

On 24 January 1502 Elizabeth and Henry were at Richmond to see Princess Margaret marry James IV. It was a grand ceremony with much of the nobility and clergy in attendance. The marriage treaty made Margaret Queen of Scotland and from that day on she was to be treated as thus. She was given her own set of apartments at Westminster and Windsor. Much to Elizabeth's relief her daughter was not to leave for Scotland until September 1503 giving her time to prepare her daughter for what lay ahead. The marriage between England and Scotland marked the beginning of the Treaty of Perpetual Peace meaning neither king could make war on the other for if they did they risked excommunication from the Pope.

Edmund de la Pole, Elizabeth's cousin, was raised to the peerage as the Earl of Suffolk, he was seen by many as the true heir to the throne and he was displeased he had not received the dukedom his father had. Disappointed and angry he left England and fled to the court of Maximillian of Austria with his brother where he started referring to himself as the white rose. Yet again Henry was having to fight off another claimant to his throne although this time he might have to fight the might of the Holy Roman Empire.

Henry must have been constantly cursing his wife's family and when William Courtenay, husband to Elizabeth's sister Katherine, was suspected of plotting with de la Pole to attack England he was arrested and placed in the Tower. As a result, he lost all his lands and income leaving Katherine and her children facing ruin. Elizabeth offered her support to her sister by giving her a place in her household, the children were already under her care which may indicate she was aware of Courtenay's betrayal. But news was coming from Ludlow of Arthur's ill heath, in early April Elizabeth went to Hampton Court, which at that time was seen as a bolt hole and not the grand palace we know of today. She went for some rest and she was back at Greenwich a few days later with Henry when the devastating news came from Ludlow that Prince Arthur was dead.

Arthur Tudor, Prince of Wales died on 2 April 1502 at the age of 15 years old, he had been married to Katherine for just six months. The news reached his parents on the night of 4 April, it was first relayed to the Privy Council who then sought out the king to break the news to him that his son and heir was dead. Henry's first reaction was to go to Elizabeth so they could grieve together, her first reaction was to take control. They were both utterly devastated by the loss but she reassured Henry they could have more sons; Henry had invested so much time and effort in training Arthur to be the perfect heir and all that stood between the loss of his dreams of a Tudor dynasty was a young boy – Prince Henry. Once Elizabeth had soothed her husband she returned to her rooms where she then broke down, her ladies were so concerned for her that they immediately sent for Henry to comfort her.

Prince Arthur had been ill for some time and had been gradually getting worse over the previous few weeks, he had been frail from birth and his cause of death has often been attributed to tuberculosis. on the 25 April his body was sailed down the River Severn to Worcester, the Earl of Surrey stood as chief mourner as he was laid to rest at Worcester Cathedral He left nothing for Katherine in his will, he left most of her personal belongings to his sister Margaret. Katherine left Ludlow and returned to London where Elizabeth warmly received her at Richmond, she would later take up residence at Croydon Palace, the Surrey residence of the Archbishop of Canterbury.

The de la Pole conspiracy continued to rage and one man executed for his part was James Tyrell. Tyrell had been previously linked to the disappearance of the Princes in the Tower and prior to his death he was examined over his involvement at the Tower, Elizabeth was in residence at the time but is unknown how much involvement she had during his interviews.

Elizabeth and Henry rarely spent any time apart since Arthur's death and soon Elizabeth was pregnant again. In July 1502 Elizabeth went with her sister Katherine to Woodstock in Oxfordshire in her first solo progress. It seems a strange time to make such a trip and she was away from Henry for over two months. It may have been a case of needing to rest and recuperate away from Henry, she had shouldered his grief as well as her own and now she was pregnant again she needed peace and quiet to grieve for herself. It is known Elizabeth was never as close to Arthur as she had been with her other children, she spent the first few months of his life separated and then he was sent to Ludlow at the age of 6, maybe she felt a certain element of guilt and she needed to process her feelings and she could only do that away from court.

Elizabeth always seems to have been apologising to Henry for the antics of her family. Katherine's husband, her de la Pole cousins and now Cecily had re-married without royal consent to a man much lower than her in rank. She had married Thomas Kyme and when Henry found out he banished her from court and confiscated her Welles lands and rents which he had previously promised her for life. We don't know exactly what Elizabeth's reaction was, whether she tried to intercede on Cecily's behalf or whether she had had enough and refused to get involved. Margaret Beaufort stepped in and offered the newlyweds the use of her home Collyweston whilst she negotiated with Henry over the Welles estates, she was successful and they were restored to Cecily. Did Elizabeth not hold as much sway as she once did with Henry or was she not happy with her sister's behaviour?

Given the loss of Arthur and the trials of another pregnancy Elizabeth and Henry's marriage seems to have been struggling, there was pressure on Elizabeth to produce a boy for Henry and her health was not as robust as it had once been and there was talk of her suffering from anaemia, which given the number of pregnancies she had gone through is understandable. Whilst she was on progress with Katherine she made many religious offerings at various shrines in the hope of a safe delivery of a son. When she returned to London she took up residence at the Tower of London, from there she went to Richmond where she spent her first Christmas without Arthur but she had his widow Katherine there as comfort. From Richmond Elizabeth sailed back down the Thames to the Tower to prepare for the birth. A monk from Westminster Abbey brought 'Our Lady's Girdle' in preparation, it was supposed to offer protection to mothers going through labour, was this a sign Elizabeth did not feel all was well and that she needed extra support?

Elizabeth went into labour two weeks early on 2 February 1503, it may not have been her intention to give birth at the Tower as there were other more suitable palaces for a queen to give birth in, in fact this would be the last royal birth to happen at the Tower of London. The baby was a girl and by an account from Thomas More, the labour was very difficult for Elizabeth. The baby was weak and was hastily christened at St Peter ad Vincula, she was named Katherine.

On the 9 February Elizabeth fell ill which caused Henry so much concern that he summoned the royal physician from Plymouth to attend the queen. Sadly, it would transpire she had developed puerperal fever and she quickly fell seriously ill. Henry could not wait for his physician to arrive, instead he called for Elizabeth's from his home in Gravesend but he arrived too late.

Elizabeth, queen of England died in the early hours of 11 February 1503 aged 37 years old. Henry was by her side when she passed and her death left him devastated, he left the funeral arrangements to his mother, Thomas Howard the Earl of Surrey and Sir Richard Guildford. He then travelled to Richmond alone to grieve in private. Baby Katharine died shortly after her mother and was buried in Westminster Abbey. The bells of St Paul's tolled out for the death of a much beloved queen as the country mourned.

After her death her body was washed and dressed in her robes of estate, she was laid out for the children, who were dressed in mourning, came to bid their beloved mother one final goodbye. Their grandmother Margaret Beaufort took control of them in the days after their mother's death which was no doubt a huge comfort for them. Her children were left shattered by their mother's death, Prince Henry was especially affected by the loss as he held his mother in such high regard and would name his daughter after her. The queen's body lay in state for eleven days in the chapel of St Peter ad Vincula, the queen's sister Katherine was the chief mourner and she stood vigil with six other ladies at all times, she was a constant presence beside her sister. The funeral was a lavish ceremony costing well in excess of one million pounds in today's money, Henry spared no expense for his wife's last state duty.

On 22 February the coffin left St Peter's draped in black velvet and adorned with a cross of white cloth of gold. At around noon it left the Tower of London on a carriage pulled by six horses draped in black velvet and Elizabeth started her final journey through the streets of London. On top of her coffin was an effigy of Elizabeth that had been dressed in her finest robes and her crown sat atop her head and she held her sceptre and rod. The journey was the same she had taken on the way to her coronation just fifteen years before. Eight ladies followed the cortege on white horses followed by many lords and the Lord Mayor of London, her four sisters followed her coffin closely. She was laid to rest in the Lady Chapel in Westminster Abbey.

Henry remained at Richmond for six weeks, it was whilst he was there that he fell ill with quinsy, a painful and dangerous condition that affects the tonsils, in fact he was so ill that many thought him to be near death. The death of his son and heir followed by his beloved wife and infant daughter had left him shattered and broken, it seemed like it was just all too much for him to bear. But he had worked so hard during his reign to establish his dynasty and with a son and two daughters left to him he had something to fight for. He re-entered public life on Palm Sunday on 15 March and attended services at St Paul's, he was still wearing his mourning robes and he looked old and frail but life had to go on for the sake of the country.

Elizabeth was mourned across Europe, known as the eldest daughter of Edward IV, sister to the princes in the tower, wife to

Henry VII, and later as the mother to Henry VIII and grandmother to Mary I and Elizabeth I. They were all remarkable people whose reigns left their mark on England but Elizabeth of York can stand proudly as her own person. She was a sweet natured, beloved queen who enjoyed good relationships with everyone she met. Her relationship with her husband has been debated down through the centuries, many say they had a loveless marriage with him being cruel and cold-hearted, a miser who ignored his wife and who preferred the opinion of his mother. But when we look at the records their marriage was far from cold, it was one of love and respect, regardless of what history may tell us. She may have been overshadowed by her descendants but she was a popular and well-loved queen.

Henry never remarried despite just having Henry as his heir, Katherine Gordon remained close but Elizabeth was his queen and no one could ever replace her in his eyes. Following Elizabeth's death, the court became a sombre and sad place to be, Henry aged and became the miserly and cruel man we know of today. He was lonely and sad; he missed his wife greatly and he could never seem to get over her death. He turned his attention to Prince Henry and began training him in the role of kingship but he became obsessed in making sure his heir remained safe and life for the lively Prince became hard and oppressive.

King Henry VII died on 21 April 1509 at Richmond Palace, his cause of death was tuberculosis. Sadly, he was not widely mourned and he was succeeded by his sole surviving son the 17-year-old King Henry VIII and as promised, he married his first love Katherine of Aragon shortly after his accession. Henry VIII was very close to his mother and he named his daughter with Anne Boleyn after her and it is often said he strived to find a wife that had the same character as his mother. He may finally have found that wife in Jane Seymour but she was sadly taken from him following childbirth, the similarities between Jane and Elizabeth are remarkable. Not many people know who Elizabeth of York was but she was a vital member of English royal history, without her the Tudor dynasty would not have become one of the cornerstones of English history it has.

Elizabeth's blood has flowed through the royal family via her daughter Queen Margaret of Scotland, her great-grandson was King James I of England and that blood runs through the veins of King Charles III to this very day.

Appendix One

The Battles of the Wars of the Roses

Below is a list of the battles that took place during the Wars of the Roses between the House of Lancaster and the House of York.

Date	**Battle**	**Winner**
22 May 1455	First of St Albans	York
23 September 1459	Blore Heath	York
12 October 1459	Ludford Bridge	Lancaster
10 July 1460	Northampton	York
30 December 1460	Wakefield	Lancaster
2 February 1461	Mortimer's Cross	York
17 February 1461	Second of St Albans	Lancaster
28 March 1461	Ferrybridge	York
29 March 1461	Towton	York
25 April 1464	Hedgeley Moor	York
15 May 1464	Hexham	York
26 July 1469	Edgecote	Warwick for Lancaster
12 March 1470	Losecote Field	York
14 April 1471	Barnet	York
4 May 1471	Tewkesbury	York
22 August 1485	Bosworth	Tudor for Lancaster
16 June 1487	Stoke	Tudor for Lancaster

Appendix Two

The Children of King Edward IV and Queen Elizabeth

Princess Elizabeth: Born on 11 February 1466 at Westminster Palace. She married Henry VII after his victory at the Battle of Bosworth which saw Elizabeth's uncle, King Richard III, killed. As Queen of England she was well loved and respected. She gave birth seven times, her children included the future Henry VIII, Queen Margaret of Scotland and Queen Mary of France. She died at the Tower of London following the birth of her daughter in February 1503, she is buried alongside her husband in a grand tomb at Westminster Abbey.

Princess Mary: Born on 11 August 1467 at Windsor Castle. Her early years were spent in the royal nursery at Sheen Palace and in May 1480 she was made a Lady of the Garter. Her health began to deteriorate at the end of 1481 and she died at Greenwich on 23 May 1482 aged 15 years old and was buried at St George's Chapel at Windsor Castle.

Princess Cecily: Born on 20 March 1469 at Westminster Palace. Initially betrothed to the heir to the Scottish throne in 1474 she was known as the Princess of Scotland; however, the betrothal was broken in 1482. Cecily then went on to marry Ralph Scrope in 1485 that was later dissolved and she then went on to marry John Welles, 1st Viscount Welles with whom she had two daughters Elizabeth and Anne. Sadly, Viscount Welles died on 9 February 1499. Cecily married for a third and final time in 1502 to commoner Thomas

Kyme with whom she had two children Richard and Margaret. The marriage was controversial and saw Cecily leave court. She died on 24 August 1507 aged 38 years old, her final resting place is thought to be either Quarr Abbey on the Isle of Wight or the Friary at Kings Langley.

King Edward V: Born 2 November 1470 at Westminster Abbey. The first-born son and heir of the king Edward was born whilst his mother and elder sisters sought sanctuary at Cheneygates. He was created Prince of Wales in June 1471 following his father's restoration to the throne. In 1473 he was sent to Ludlow Castle where he established his own household, his father created him Earl of Pembroke in 1479. He was betrothed to Anne of Brittany in 1480. When his father died suddenly on 9 April 1483, Edward acceded to the throne as King Edward V. On his journey back from Ludlow to London his party was intercepted by those of his uncle Richard, Duke of Gloucester. Richard took Edward into his care and placed him in the Tower of London to prepare for his coronation. Edward disappeared from the Tower sometime in 1483 and was never seen alive again. He was 12 years old. His place of burial is unknown but it is thought his remains were discovered alongside his brother at the Tower of London in July 1674 and they were interred in a casket at Westminster Abbey. It has never been confirmed that they are the bones of Edward and Richard.

Princess Margaret: Born 10 April 1472 at Winchester Castle, she sadly died on 11 December 1472 aged just 8 months old and was buried at Westminster Abbey

Prince Richard, Duke of York: Born 17 August 1473 at Shrewsbury he was created the Duke of York in May 1474 and Earl of Nottingham on 12 June 1476. At the age of 4 he married 5-year-old heiress Anne Mowbray, 8th Countess of Norfolk. He was sent to the Tower of London to join his elder brother Edward as he prepared for his coronation. He disappeared sometime in 1483 whilst at the Tower of London, he was never seen alive again and was aged 9 years old.

Princess Anne: Born 2 November 1475 at Westminster Palace. At the age of 4 she was betrothed to Philip, the son of Archduke Maximillian of Austria but that was broken off when her father died. In 1484 she was betrothed to Thomas Howard, the son and heir of the Earl of Surrey and future Duke of Norfolk. They were married on 4 February 1495 at Westminster Abbey. The marriage was an unhappy one and none of their children survived long past their birth. Ann struggled with ill health and died on 23 November 1511 aged 36 years old, she was initially buried at Thetford Priory but was later reburied at the Church of St Michael the Archangel at Framlingham.

Prince George, Duke of Bedford: Born March 1477 at Windsor Castle. He was appointed Lord Lieutenant of Ireland in 1478. George died in March 1479 aged 2 years old and was buried at St George's Chapel, Windsor Castle.

Princess Catherine: Born 14 August 1479 at Greenwich. In 1495 she married William Courtenay the son and heir of the Earl of Devon who was arrested after being involved in a plot with Edmund de la Pole to remove Henry VII from his throne. They had three children, Henry, Edward and Margaret, their welfare was passed over to Lady Margaret Coton and the queen, her sister, paid for their upkeep. Courtenay died on 9 June 1511. Catherine died on 15 November 1527 at the age of 38 years old and was buried at St Peter's Church, Tiverton.

Princess Bridget: Born 10 November 1480 at Eltham Palace. She was considered for holy orders almost from birth and entered Dartford Priory before 1489. She died sometime before December 1507 aged around 26 years old and is buried at Dartford Priory.

Appendix Three

Titulus Regis

On 26 June 1483 Richard, Duke of Gloucester ascended the throne of England as King Richard III. The document below which was issued in 1484 establishes the basis on which Richard claimed his throne. The marriage of King Edward VI and Elizabeth Woodville was invalid and therefore the children rendered illegitimate.

Titulus Regis

Where late heretofore, that is to say, before the consecracion, coronacion and inthronizacion of oure Souveraign Lord the King Richard the Thirde, a rolle of perchement, conteignyng in writeing certeine articles of the tenour undre writen, on the behalve and in the name of the thre Estates of this Reame of Englond, that is to wite, of the lords spirituells and temporalls, and of the Commons by many and diverse lords spirituells and temporalls, and other nobles and notable personnes of the Commons in grete multitude, was presented and actualy delivered unto oure said Souveraine Lord the King, to th'entent and effect expressed at large in the same rolle; to the which rolle, and to the consideracions and instant peticion comprized in the same, our said Souveraine Lord, for the public wele and tranquillite of this land, benignely assented.

Nowe forasmuch as neither the said three Estats, neither the said personnes, which in thair name presented and delivered, as is abovesaid the said rolle unto oure said Souverain Lord the King, were assembled in fourme of Parliament; by occasion whereof, diverse doubts, questions and ambiguitiees, been moved and engendered in the myndes of diverse personnes, as it is said: Therfore, to the perpetuall memorie of the trouth, and declaration of th'same, bee it ordeigned, provided and stablisshed in this present Parliament, that the tenour of the said rolle, with all the contynue of the same, presented, as is abovesaid, and delivered to oure before said Souverain Lord the King, in the name, and on the behalve of the said three Estates out of Parliament, now by the same three Estates assembled in this present Parliament, and by auctorite of the same, bee ratifyed, enrolled, recorded, approved and auctorized, into removyng the occasion of doubtes and ambiguitees, and to all other lawfull effect that shall mowe thereof ensue; soo that all things said, affirmed, specifyed, desired and remembered in the said rolle, and in the tenour of the same underwritten, in the name of the said three Estates, to the effect expressed in the same rolle, bee of like effect, vertue and force, as if all the same things had ben soo affirmed, specifyed, desired and remembred in a full Parliament, and by auctorite of the same accepted and approved. The tenoure of the said rolle of parchement, whereof above is made mencione, foloweth and is such To the High and Myghty Prince Richard Duc of Gloucester

Please if youre Noble Grace to understande the consideracion, election, and petition underwritten of us the lords spiritual and temporal and commons of this reame of England, and thereunto agreably to geve your assent, to the common and public wele of this lande, to the comforte and gladnesse of all the people of the same.

Furst, we considre how that heretofore in tyme passeed this lande many years stode in great prosperite, honoure, and tranquillitie, which was caused forsomuch as the kings then reignyng used and followed the advice and counsaill of certaine lords spirituelx and temporelx, and othre personnes of approved sadnesse, prudence, policie, and experience, dreading God, and having tendre zele and affection to indifferent ministration of justice, and to the comon and politique wele of the land; then our Lord God was dres, luffed loved, and honoured; then within the land was peace and tranquillite, and among neghbors concorde and charite; then the malice of outward enemyes was myghtily repressed and resisted, and the land honrably defended with many grete and glorious victories; then the entrecourse of merchandizes was largely used and exercised; by which things above remembred, the land was greatly enriched, soo that as wele the merchants and artificers as other poor people, laborying for their lyvyng in diverse occupations, had competent gayne to the sustentation of povertie. But afterward, when that such as had the rule and governaunce of this land, delting in adulation and flattery and lede by sensuality and concuposcence, folowed the counsaill of good, vertuous, and prudent personnes such as above be remembred, the prosperite of this lande daillie decreased, soo that felicite was turned into miserie, and prosperite into adversite, and the ordre of polecye, and of the law of God and man, confounded; whereby it is likely this reame to falle into extreme miserie and desolation, – which god defende, – without due provision of convenable remedie bee had in this behalfe in all godly hast.

Over this, amonges other thinges, more specially we consider howe that the tyme of the raigne of Kyng Edward IV., late decessed, after the ungracious pretensed marriage, as all England hath cause to say, made betwixt the said King Edward and Elizabeth sometyme wife to Sir John Grey, Knight, late nameing herself and many years heretofore Queene of England, the ordre of all pollteque rule was perverted, the law of God and of Gode's church, and also the lawes of nature and of Englond, and also the laudable customes and liberties of the same, wherein every Englishman is inheritor, broken, subverted, and contempned, against all reason and justice, so that this land was ruled by self-will and pleasure, feare and drede, all manner of equitie and lawes layd apart and despised, whereof ensued many inconvenients and mischiefs, as murdres, estortions, and oppressions, namely of poor and impotent people, soo that no man was sure of his lif, land,, ne lyvelode, ne if his wif, doughter, ne servaunt, every good maiden and woman standing in drede to be ravished and defouled. And besides this, what discords, inward battailes, effusion of Christian men's blode, and namely, by the destruction of the noble blode of this londe, was had and comitted within the same, it is evident and notarie through all this reaume unto the grete sorrowe and heavynesse of all true Englishmen. And here also we considre howe that the said pretensed marriage, bitwixt the above named King Edward and Elizabeth Grey, was made of grete presumption, without the knowying or assent of the lords of this lond, and alsoe by sorcerie and wichecrafte, committed by the said Elizabeth and her moder, Jaquett Duchess of Bedford, as the common opinion of the people and the publique voice and fame is through all this land; and hereafter, if and as the case shall require, shall pretenced marriage was made privatly and secretly, without edition of banns, in a private chamber, a profane place, and not openly in the face of the church, aftre the lawe of Godds churche but contrarie thereunto, and the laudable custome of the Churche of England. And howe also, that at the tyme of contract of the same pretensed marriage, and bifore and longe tyme after the said King Edward was and stoode marryed and trouth plyght to oone Dame Elianor Butteler, doughter of the old Earl of Shrewesbury, with whom the saide King Edward had made a precontracte of matrimonie, longe tyme bifore he made the said pretensed marriage with the said Elizabeth Grey in manner and fourme aforesaide. Which premises being true, as in veray trouth they been true, it appeareth and followeth evidently, that the said King Edward duryng his lyfe and the said Elizabeth lived together sinfully and dampnably in adultery, against the lawe of God and his church; and therefore now marvaile that the souverain lord and head of this londe, being of such ungodly disposicion, and provokyng the ire and indignation of oure Lorde God, such haynous mischiefs and inconvenients as is above remembered, were used and committed in the reame amongst the subjects. Also it appeareth evidently and followeth that all th issue and children of the said king beene bastards, and unable to inherite or to clayme anything by inheritance, by the lawe and custome of England.

Moreover we consider howe that aftreward, by the thre estates of this reame assembled in a parliament holden at Westminster the xvjth yere of the regne of the said King Edward the iiijth, he then being in possession of coroune and roiall estate, by an acte made in the same parliaent, George Duc of Clarence, brother to the same King Edward now decessed, was convicted and attainted of high treason; and in the same acte is conteigned more at large. Because and by reason whereof all the issue of the said George was and is disabled and barred of all right and clayme that in any wise they might have or challenge by enheritence to the crowne and roiall dignitie of this reame, by the auncien lawe and custome of this same reame.

Over this we consider howe that ye be the undoubted sonne and heire of Richard late Duke of Yorke verray enheritour to the said crowne and dignitie roiall and as in ryght Kyng of Englond by way if enheritaunce and that at this time the premisses duely considered that is noon other person lyvyng but ye only, that by right may clayme the said coroune and dignitie roiall, by way of enheritaunce, and how that ye be born within this lande, by reason whereofm as we deme in our myndes, ye be more naturally enclyned to the prosperite and comen wele of the same: and all the three estates of the land have, and may have more certain knowledge of your birth and fillation above said. Wee considre also, the greate wytte, prudence, justice, princely courage, and the memorable and laudable acts in diverse battalls which we of this same reame, and also the greate noblesse an excellence of your byrth and blode as of hym that is descended of the thre most royal houses in Christendom, that is to say, England, Fraunce, and Hispaine.

Whereof these presmises by us diligently considered, we desyring affectuously the peas, tranquilitie and wele publique of this lande, and the reducion of the same to the auncien honourable estate and prosperite, and havyng in your greate prudence, justice, princely courage and excellent virtue, singular confidence, have chosen in all that in us is and by this our wrytyng choise you, high and myghty Prynce into our Kyng and soveraine lorde & c., to whom we knowe for certayn it appartaneth of enheritaunce so to be choosen. And hereupon we humbly desire, pray, and require your said noble grace, that accordinge to this election of us the three estates of this lande, as by your true enheritaunce ye will accept and take upon you the said crowne and royall dignitie with all things thereunto annexed and apperteynyng as to you of right belongyng as well by enheritaunce as by lawfull election, and in caas ye do so we promitte to serve and to assiste your highnesse, as true and faithfull subjietz and liegemen and to lyve and dye with you in this matter and every other just quarrel. For certainly we bee determined rather to aventure and comitte us to the perill of our lyfs and jopardye of deth, than to lyve in suche thraldome and bondage as we have lyved long tyme heretofore, oppressed and injured by new extorcions and imposicions, agenst the lawes of God and man, and the liberte, old police and lawes of this reame wherein every Englishman is inherited. Oure Lorde God Kyng of all Kyngs by whose infynte goodnesse and eternall providence all thyngs been pryncypally gouvered in this worlde lighten your soule, and graunt you grace to do, as well in this matter as in all other, all that may be accordyng to his will and pleasure, and to the comen and publique wele of this land, so that after great cloudes troubles, stormes, and tempests, the son of justice and of grace may shyne upon us, to the comforte and gladnesse of all true Englishmen.

Albeit that the right, title, and estate, whiche oure souverain lorde the Kyng Richard III. Hath to and in the crown and roiall dignite of this reame of England, with all thyngs thereunto annexed and appertynyng, been juste and lawefull, as grounded upon the lawes of God and of nature, and also upon the auncien lawes and laudable customes of this said reame, and so taken and reputed by all suche personnes as ben lerned in the abovesaide lawes and custumes. Yet, neverthelesse, forasmoche as it is considred that the moste parte of the people of his lande is not suffisiantly lerned in the abovesaid lawes and custumes whereby the trueth and right in this behalf of liklyhode may be hyd, and not clerely knowen to all the people and thereupon put in doubt and question: And over this howe that the courte of Parliament is of suche autorite, and the people of this lande of suche nature and desposicion, as experience teacheth that manifestation and declaration of any trueth or right made by the thre estats of this reame assembled in parliament, and by auctorite of the same maketh before all other thyng. Moost faith and certaintie; and quietyng men's myndes, remoweth the occasion of all doubts ans seditious language:

Therefore at the request, and by the assent of the three estates of this reame, that is to say, the lords spirituelx and temporalx and coments of this lande, assembled in this present parliament by auctorite of the same, bee it pronounced, decreed and declared, that oure saide souveraign lorde the kinge was and is veray and undoubted kyng of this reame of Englond; with all thyngs thereunto within this same reame, and without it annexed unite and apperteynyng, as well by right of consanguinite and enheritance as by lawful election, consecration and coronacion. And over this, that at the request, and by the assent and autorite abovesaide bee it ordeigned, enacted and established that the said crowne and roiall dignitie of this reame and the inheritaunce of the same, and other thyngs thereunto within the same reame or without it annexed, unite, and now apperteigning, rest and abyde in the personne of oure said souveraign lord the kyng duryng his lyfe, and after his decesse in his heires of his body begotten, And in especiall, at the request and by the assent and decesse in his heires of his body begotten, And in especiall, at the request and by the assent and auctorite above said, bee it ordeigned, enacted, established, pronounced, decreed and declared that the high and excellent Prince Edward, sone of oure said souveraign lorde the kyng, to succeed to hym in the abovesayde crown and roiall dignitie, with all thyngs as is aforesaid thereunto unite annexed and apperteignyng, to have them after the decesse of our saide souveraign lorde the kyng to hym and to his heires of his body lawfully begotten.

Appendix Four

The Annulment of the *Titulus Regis* by Henry VII

This is the bill that was passed by King Henry VII in the first Parliament of his reign in November 1485. The bill annuls the previous act that was passed during the reign of King Richard III which established his right to the crown of England. King Henry VII had requested all copies of the *Titulus Regis* to be destroyed, this order was not obeyed leaving the original copy available.

Annulment of Titulus Regius

Where before this time, Richard, late duke of Gloucester, and afterwards in deed and not by right king of England, called Richard III, caused a false and seditious bill of false and malicious contrivance to be put to him, against all good and true order, which bill begins thus: 'May it please your noble grace to understand the considerations, election and petition written below', etc. Afterwards, this bill, with all its contents, by authority of parliament held in the first year of the usurped reign of the said late King Richard III (1484), was ratified, enrolled, recorded, approved and authorised, as more fully appears in the same. The king, at the special request, desire and prayer of the lords spiritual and temporal and of the commons assembled in this present parliament, wills that it be ordained, decreed and enacted, by the advice of the said lords spiritual and temporal and the commons assembled in this present parliament, and by authority of the same, that the said bill, act and ratification, with all the details and consequences of the same bill and act, for its false and seditious contrivance and untruth, be void, annulled, repealed, cancelled and of no effect or force. And that it be ordained by the said authority that the said bill be cancelled and destroyed, and that the said act, record and enrolment be taken and removed from the roll and records of the said parliament of the said late king, and burnt and entirely destroyed, And moreover, be it ordained by the same authority that any person who has any copy or remembrance of the said bill or act shall bring the to the chancellor of England at the time, or destroy the entirely in some other way, before next Easter, upon pain of imprisonment and of making fine and ransom to the king at his will, so that all the things said and rehearsed in the said bill and act may be forever out of memory and forgotten. And moreover, be it ordained by the said authority that this act, or anything contained it, be not harmful or prejudicial to the act establishing the crown of England on the king and the heirs begotten of his body.

Appendix Five

Ordinances of a Royal Birth by Lady Margaret Beaufort

Below is the Ordinances written by Margaret Beaufort, Countess of Richmond and Derby, as to what preparation is to be made against the deliverance of a Queen. They were the rules that were to be adhered to during a royal birth, they were written especially for Elizabeth during her first pregnancy.

Taken from *Joannis Lelandi antiquarii De rebus Britannicis collectanea Third Volume, p279 onwards*

Her Highnes Pleasure beinge understoode in what Chamber she will be delivered in, the same must be hanged with riche Clothe of Arras, Sydes, rowffe, Windowes and all, excepte one Windowe, which must be hanged so as she may have light when it pleasethe her. Then must there be set a Royall Bedde, and the Flore layed all over and over with Carpets, and a Cupboard covered with the same Suyte that the Chamber is hanged withall. Also there must be ordayned a faier Pallet, and all Things appertayninge therunto, and a riche Sparner hanginge over the same. And that Daye that the Queene (in good Tyme) will take her Chamber, the Chappell where her Highnes will receave and heare Devine Service, must be well and worshipfully arrayed. Also the greate Chamber must be hanged with riche Arras, with a Clothe and Chaire of Estate, and Quishins [cushions] thereto belonginge, the Place under and aboute the same beinge well encarped. Where the Queene (comminge from the Chappell with her Lords and Ladyes of Estate) may, either standinge or sittinge, at her Pleasure, receave spices and wyne. And the next Chamber betwixt the greate Chamber and the Queenes Chamber to be well and worshipfully hanged; which done, Two of the greatest Estats shall leade her to her Chamber, where they shall take their leave of her. Then all the Ladyes and Gentilwomen to goe in with her, and none to come unto the greate Chamber but Women; and Women to be made all Manner of Officers, as Butlers, Panters, sewers, & c. and all Manner of Officers shall bringe them all neadfull Thinges unto the greate Chamber Dore, and the Women Officers shall receave it there of them'.

Appendix Six

The Song of Lady Bessy

Below is a short excerpt from the *Song of Lady Bessy*. This extract focuses on the rumours that King Richard III wanted to poison his wife Anne Neville and make Elizabeth his queen. Elizabeth is pleading with Lord Stanley to help her and the Earl of Richmond to marry. This extract is taken from *The Most Pleasant Song of Lady Bessy The Eldest Daughter of King Edward the Fourth and how she married King Henry the Seventh of the House of Lancaster.* This edition came with notes by Thomas Heywood and was published in 1829 by Richard Taylor of London.

Oh father Stanley, to you I call,
For the love of God remember thee,
Since my father King Edward, that King royal,
At Westminster on his death bed lee,
He called to him my unckle Richard,
So he did Robert of Brakenbury,
And James Terrill he was the third
He sent them to Ludlow in the West Countrey
To fetch the Duke of York and the Duke of Clarence,
These two Lords born of a high degree;
The Duke of York should have been Prince And King after my father free
But a balle - full game was then among,
When they doomed these two Lords to dye
They had neither justice nor right, but had great wrong,

Alack! it was the more pitty.
Neither were they burried in St. Maries,
In church or church - yard,
of holy place Alas! they had dolefull destines,
Hard was their chance, worse was their disgrace,
Therefore help, good father Stanley, while you have space,
For the love of God and mild Mary,
Or else in time to come you shall, alas!
Remember the words of Lady Bessy.
Good lady Bessy, be content,
For tho' your words be never so sweet,
If King Richard knew, you must be shent,
And perchance cast into prison deep;
Then had you cause to waile and weep
And wring your hands with heavy cheat
Therefore, good Lady, I you beseek To move me no more in this matter.

Oh, good father Stanley,
Listen now and Heare is no more but you and I,
King Edward that was my father dear,
On whose estate God had mercy,
In Westminster as he did stand On a certain day in a study,
A book of reason he had in his hand,
And so sore his study he did apply,
That his tender tears fell on the ground,
All men might see that stood him by;
There were both Earls and Lords of land,
But none of them durst speak but I.
I came before my father the King,
And kneeled down upon my knee I desired him lowly of his blessing,

And full soon he gave it unto me And in his arms he could me thring,
And set me in a window so high He spake to me full sore weeping;
These were the words he said to me Daughter,
As thou wilt have my blessing,
Do as I shall councell thee;
And to my words give good listning,
For one day they may pleasure thee Here is a book of reason; keep it well,
As you will have the love of me;
Neither to any creature do it tell,
Nor let no liveing Lord it see,
Except it be to the Lord Stanley.

The which I love full heartiley All the matter to him shew you may,
For he and his thy help must be; As soon as the truth to him is shown,
Unto your words he will agree For their shall never son off my body begotten,
That shall be crowned after me;
But you shall be Queen and wear the crown,
So do thee expresse the prophecye .
He gave me tax and toland, And also diamonds to my degree,
To gett me a Prince when it pleaseth Christ The world is not as it will be,
Therefore, good father Stanley,
Grant my request For the love of God I desire thee;
All is at your commandment down in the west Both Knight and Squire and the Commentie;
You may choose then where you like best,
I have enough both of gold and fee;
I want nothing but the strength of men,
And good captains two or three .

Go away, Bessy, the Lord said then;
To this will I never agree,
For women oft time cannot faine,
These words they be but vain glory;
For, and I should treason begin Against King Richard his royalty,
In every street within London The Eagle's foot should be pulled down,
And as yet in his great favour I am,
But then should I loose my great renowne,
I should be called traitor thro' the same Full soon in every markett towne,
That were great shame to me and my name,
I had rather spend ten thousand pounde .

Oh, father Stanley, to you I make my moane,
For the love of God remember thee;
It is not three days past and gone Since my unckle Richard sent after me,
A Batchelor, and a bold Baron, A Doctor of Divinitye,
And bad that I should to his chamber gone;
His love and his leman that I shoud bee,
And the Queen that was his wedded feere,
He would her poyson and putt away,
So woud be his son and his heir Christ knoweth he is a proper boy.
Yet had I rather burn in a tunne On the Tower Hill that is so high,
Or that I woud to his chamber come His love and his leman will I not be,
I had rather be draw' n with wild horses five Through every street of that citty,
Or that good woman should loose her life,
Good father, for the love of mee.

I am his brother's daughter dear He is my uncle; it is no nay,
Or ever I would be his wedded feer With sharp swords I will me slay;

At his biding if I were then, And follow'd also his cruel intent,
I were well worthy to suffer pain And in a fire for to be brent.
Therefore, good father Stanley, some pitty take On the Earle Richmond and me,
And the rather for my father' s sake Which gave thee the Isle of Man so free;
He crowned the with a crown of lead,
He holpe the first to that degree,
He set thee the crown upon thy head,
And made thee the lord of that country,
That time you promised my father dear,
To him to be both true and just,
And now you stand in a disweare,
Oh Jesu Christ, who may men trust!

Bibliography

Primary Sources

Lelandi, J. *Antiquarii De rebus Britannicis Collectanea Third Volume, p279 onwards.* Accessed via Google Books on 21 July 2023

Heywood, T. *The Most Pleasant Song of Lady Bessy The Eldest Daughter of King Edward the Fourth and How She Married King Henry the Seventh of the House of Lancaster. (*Richard Taylor, London, 1829)

Secondary Sources

Amin, N. *Henry VII and the Tudor Pretenders: Simnel, Warbeck and Warwick,* (Amberley Publishing, Stroud, 2022)

Ashdown-Hill, J. *Richard III's 'Beloved Cousyn' John Howard and the House of York,* (The History Press, Stroud, 2015)

Borman, T. *The Private Lives of the Tudors: Uncovering the Secrets of Britain's Greatest Dynasty,* (Hodder & Stoughton, London, 2016)

Borman, T. *Henry VIII and the Men who Made Him*, (Hodder & Stoughton, London, 2019)

Carson, A. *Richard III: The Maligned King*, (The History Press, Stroud, 2013)

Dale, I. *Kings and Queens, 1200 Years of English and British Monarchs*, (Hodder & Stoughton, London, 2023)

De Lisle, L. *Tudor, The Family Story*, (Vintage, London, 2014)

Hodder, S. *The Woodville Women, 100 Years of Plantagenet and Tudor History* (Pen and Sword, Barnsley, 2022)

Horrox, R. *Richard III* (Penguin Monarchs Series, Penguin, London, 2022)

Lewis, M. *The Survival of the Princes in the Tower: Murder, Mystery and Myth* (The History Press, Stroud, 2018

Lewis, M. *Richard III: Loyalty Bounds Me,* (Amberley, Stroud, 2018)

Licence, A. *Edward IV & Elizabeth Woodville: A True Romance*, (Amberley, Stroud, 2016)

Licence, A. *In Bed with the Tudors: The Sex Lives of a Dynasty from Elizabeth of York to Elizabeth I,* (Amberley, Stroud, 2013)

Licence, A. *Elizabeth of York: Forgotten Tudor Queen*, (Amberley, Stroud, 2014)

MacGibbon, D. *Elizabeth Woodville: A Life,* (Amberley, Stroud, 2014)

Penn, T. *The Brothers York: An English Tragedy*, (Penguin, London, 2020)

Russell, G. *The Palace, From the Tudors to the Windsors 500 Years of History at Hampton Court,* (William Collins, London, 2023)

Weir, A. *Elizabeth of York: The First Tudor Queen,* (Vintage, London, 2014)

Weir, A. Lancaster & York: The Wars of the Roses, (Vintage, London, 2009)

Weir, A. *Richard III & The Princes in the Tower*, (Vintage, London 2014)

Wooding, L. *Tudor England: A History*, (Yale University Press, London, 2022)

Index

Alcock, J, Bishop of York, 117
Anne of York, 39, 51, 99, 121
Anjou, Margaret, 4, 22, 24-5, 28-9
Argentine, Dr John, 117
Arthur, Prince of Wales, 97-100, 104-5, 112, 117, 120-1, 124, 132, 135-8
Astwood, Thomas, 132-3

Beaufort, Lady Margaret, 57, 67-9, 78, 84-7, 90, 96, 99, 104, 108-9, 119, 125, 131, 140-1
Berners, Lady Margaret, 8, 17
Berners, Sir Richard, 8
Bourchier, Thomas, Archbishop of Canterbury, 59
Brampton, Sir Edward, 76, 114-5
Brandon, Sir William, 82
Bray, Reginald, 69
Brereton, Humphrey, 79
Bridget of York, 19, 40, 31, 111
Burdet, 44-5
Burgh, Sir Thomas, 22
Butler, Eleanor, 60, 63
Butler, Thomas, Earl of Ormond, 110

Caerlon, Dr Lewis, 68
Cecily of York, 17, 42, 75, 99, 107, 111
Charles the Bold, Duke of Burgundy, 10, 28, 43
Charles, Dauphin of France, 38
Charles VIII, King of France, 116
Clarence, George, Duke of, 3, 9-13, 15-6, 20-2, 24-5, 27-8, 31-2, 41, 43, 45-7, 54, 61, 66
Cleymound, Robert, 132
Cobbe, Margaret, 6, 26, 37
Courtenay, William, 111, 122, 126, 138

Darcy, Elizabeth, 98

Eastrey, John, 27, 56
Edmund, Earl of Rutland, 41
Edward, Earl of Warwick, 46, 80, 85, 102-3, 111, 132-5
Edward IV, King of England, 1-2, 7, 9-13, 15-7, 19, 22, 24-5, 28-30, 33, 37-8, 49, 51, 53, 56, 58, 64, 87, 113, 117, 121
Edward of Middleham, 72

Edward of Westminster, 24, 29, 42
Elizabeth of York, Queen of England, 6-8, 13, 18-20, 23-5, 30-1, 33, 35-8, 45, 47, 49, 50, 52-3, 56-7, 62, 67-71, 73-6, 78, 80, 85-91, 94-5, 102, 106, 108, 113, 118, 125, 129, 131-3, 135-6, 138-144

Ferdinand of Aragon, 113, 121, 132
Fitzalan, Thomas, Lord Maltravers, 4, 117
Fitzgerald, Gerald, Earl of Kildare, 117

George, Duke of Bedford, 39, 50, 66
Goddard, William, 44
Gordon, Katherine, 121, 126-8, 143
Gould, John, 26, 37
Grey Richard, 1, 55, 61
Grey, Thomas, Marquess of Dorset, 1, 69, 100, 117
Greystoke, Elizabeth, Lady Scrope, 26-7
Gruuthuse, Louis de, Earl of Winchester, 37
Guildford, Sir Richard, 141

Haite, Sir Richard, 55, 57
Halliwell, Sir John, 85
Hastings, Sir William, 44-5, 58
Henry, VI, King of England, 1, 4, 9, 22, 25-7, 31, 46
Henry VII, King of England, 67-72, 74-7, 80-8, 90-2, 94-6, 102, 105-6, 113, 115-6, 124-5, 129, 131, 133, 136, 141, 143
Henry, Prince, *later Henry VIII*, 113, 118, 126, 142-3
Howard, Lord Thomas, 75, 121, 141

Isabella of Castille, 113, 121

Jacquetta of Luxembourg, 1, 4, 7, 25
James III, King of Scotland, 50, 52
James IV, King of Scotland, 121, 124, 131, 138
John of Gloucester, 80

Katherine of Aragon, Infanta of Spain, 113, 121, 131-2, 135-7, 139, 141, 143
Katherine of York, 40, 51
Kyme, Sir Thomas, 75, 140

Louis XI, King of France, 22, 24, 38, 44, 50

Mancini, 47
Margaret, Duchess of Burgundy, 10, 43-4, 48, 52, 103, 115-6, 119

Margaret Tudor, 124, 131, 138-9
Mary Tudor, 123, 134
Mary of York, 17, 38, 51, 66
Maximillian I, Holy Roman Emperor, 117, 138
Milling, Thomas, 26-7, 37
More, Thomas, 141
Morton, John, Archbishop of Canterbury, 108
Mowbray, Anne, 42

Nestfield, John, 72
Neville, Anne, Duchess of Gloucester, *later Queen of England*, 11, 41-2, 71-3, 75
Neville, Cecily, Duchess of York, 7, 10, 29, 47, 72, 118
Neville, George, Archbishop of York, 7, 12
Neville, George, Duke of Bedford, 21, 25
Neville, Isabel, Duchess of Isabel, 43
Neville, John, Earl of Northumberland, *later Marquess of Montagu,* 21, 25, 29
Neville, Richard, Earl of Warwick, 3, 7, 9-16, 20-2, 24-9, 39
Neville, Thomas, the Bastard of Fauconberg, 30
Percy, Henry, Earl of Northumberland, 15
Philip of Burgundy, 50-1, 116
Plantagenet, Arthur, 110
Plantagenet, Elizabeth, Duchess of Suffolk, 39
Plantagenet, Margaret, *later Countess of Salisbury,* 80, 85, 107, 111
Pole, de la, Edmund, Earl of Suffolk, 138
Pole, de la, John, Earl of Lincoln, 103, 105

Richard, Duke of Gloucester, *later King Richard III of England*, 9, 25, 31, 42, 54-9, 61-2, 65-7, 70-2, 74, 76-8, 86, 92, 102, 114
Richard, Duke of York, 10, 41
Richard, Duke of York *(Prince in the Tower)*, 39, 56, 58-9, 114
Robin of Redesdale, 12

Savage, John, 79
Simnel, Lambert, 102-3, 105, 115, 129
Sirego, de, Dr Dominic, 26, 37
Skelton, John, 124
Stafford, Henry, Duke of Buckingham, 4, 55, 62-3, 65, 67, 69-70
Stanley, George, Lord Strange, 82

Stanley, Thomas, Earl of Derby, 28, 58, 70, 78-9, 99, 119
Stillington, Robert, Bishop of Bath & Wells, 60

Talbot, Gilbert, 79
Thomas, Gruffydd ap Rhys ap, 117
Tudor, Edmund, 84, 131
Tudor, Jasper, 84, 108, 117
Twynne, Ankarette, 46, 45
Tyrell, Sir James, 64-5, 139

Vaughan, Sir Thomas, 55, 61
Vere, John de, Earl of Oxford, 81, 99

Walters, Lucy, 110
Warbeck, Perkin, 64, 114-6, 118, 121, 124-9, 131, 133-4
Welles, John, Viscount Welles, 75
Welles, Sir Robert, 22
Willoughby, Sir Robert, 85
Woodville, Anthony, Earl Rivers, 36, 54-6, 6
Woodville, Elizabeth, Queen of England, 1-2, 7-8, 13-5, 17, 19, 21, 32, 50-1, 60-1, 72, 88, 91, 99-101, 109
Woodville, John, 14
Woodville Katherine, Duchess of Bedford, 4, 88, 107, 121
Woodville, Lionel, Bishop of Salisbury, 69, 99
Woodville, Margaret, 4
Woodville, Richard, Baron Rivers, 1, 4, 14, 29